W9-CNO-312

JUL
2004

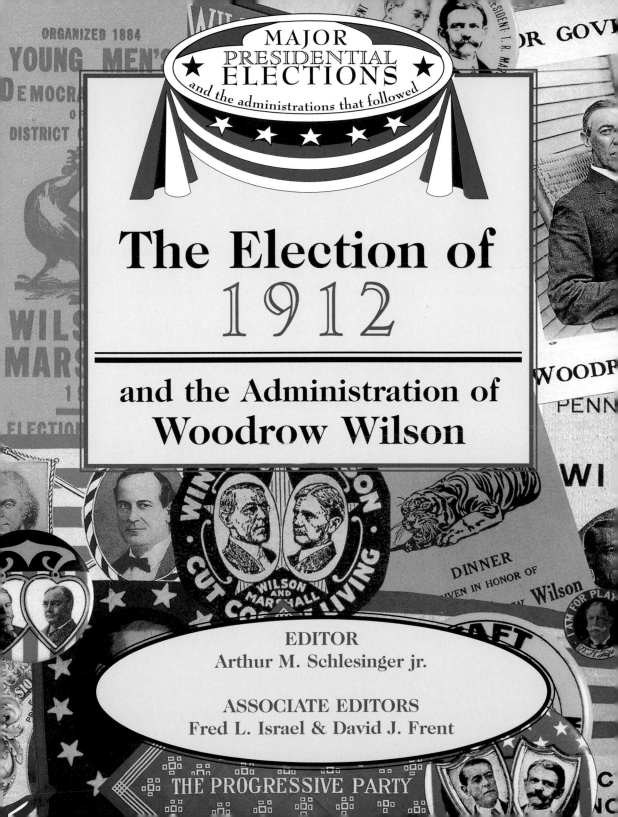

MAJOR PRESIDENTIAL ELECTIONS
and the administrations that followed

The Election of
1912
and the Administration of
Woodrow Wilson

EDITOR
Arthur M. Schlesinger jr.

ASSOCIATE EDITORS
Fred L. Israel & David J. Frent

The Elections of 1789 & 1792 and the Administration of George Washington

The Election of 1800 and the Administration of Thomas Jefferson

The Election of 1828 and the Administration of Andrew Jackson

The Election of 1840 and the Harrison/Tyler Administrations

The Election of 1860 and the Administration of Abraham Lincoln

The Election of 1876 and the Administration of Rutherford B. Hayes

The Election of 1896 and the Administration of William McKinley

The Election of 1912 and the Administration of Woodrow Wilson

The Election of 1932 and the Administration of Franklin D. Roosevelt

The Election of 1948 and the Administration of Harry S. Truman

The Election of 1960 and the Administration of John F. Kennedy

The Election of 1968 and the Administration of Richard Nixon

The Election of 1976 and the Administration of Jimmy Carter

The Election of 1980 and the Administration of Ronald Reagan

The Election of 2000 and the Administration of George W. Bush

MAJOR PRESIDENTIAL ELECTIONS and the administrations that followed

The Election of
1912

and the Administration of Woodrow Wilson

EDITOR

Arthur M. Schlesinger, jr.
Albert Schweitzer Chair in the Humanities
The City University of New York

ASSOCIATE EDITORS

Fred L. Israel
Department of History
The City College of New York

David J. Frent
The David J. and Janice L. Frent
Political Americana Collection

Mason Crest Publishers
Philadelphia

Produced by OTTN Publishing, Stockton, New Jersey

Mason Crest Publishers
370 Reed Road
Broomall PA 19008
www.masoncrest.com

Research Consultant: Patrick R. Hilferty
Editorial Assistant: Jane Ziff

First printing

1 3 5 7 9 8 6 4 2

Library of Congress Cataloging-in-Publication Data

The election of 1912 and the administration of Woodrow Wilson / editor, Arthur M. Schlesinger,
Jr.; associate editors, Fred L. Israel & David J. Frent.
    p.   cm. — (Major presidential elections and the administrations that followed)
Summary: A discussion of the presidential election of 1912 and the subsequent administration of
Woodrow Wilson, based on source documents.
   Includes bibliographical references and index.
   ISBN 1-59084-358-4
1. Presidents—United States—Election—1912—Juvenile literature. 2. Presidents—United
States—Election—1912—Sources—Juvenile literature. 3. Wilson, Woodrow, 1856-1924—
Juvenile literature. 4. United States—Politics and government—1913-1921—Juvenile literature.
5. United States—Politics and government—1913-1921—Sources—Juvenile literature.
[1. Presidents—Election—1912. 2. Wilson, Woodrow, 1856-1924. 3. Elections.
4. United States—Politics and government—1913-1921.]
I. Schlesinger, Arthur Meier, 1917-   . II. Israel, Fred L. III. Frent, David J. IV. Series.
E765.E43 2002
973.91'3—dc21

2002011264

Publisher's note: all quotations in this book come from original sources, and contain the spelling and grammatical inconsistencies of the original text.

Table of Contents

★ INTRODUCTION ★
Arthur M. Schlesinger, Jr.

America suffers from a sort of intermittent fever—what one may call a quintan ague. Every fourth year there come terrible shakings, passing into the hot fit of the presidential election; then follows what physicians call "the interval"; then again the fit.

—James Bryce, *The American Commonwealth* (1888)

Running for president is the central rite in the American political order. It was not always so. *Choosing* the chief magistrate had been the point of the quadrennial election from the beginning, but it took a long while for candidates to *run* for the highest office in the land; that is, to solicit, visibly and actively, the support of the voters. These volumes show through text and illustration how those aspiring to the White House have moved on from ascetic self-restraint to shameless self-merchandising. This work thereby illuminates the changing ways the American people have conceived the role of their President. I hope it will also recall to new generations some of the more picturesque and endearing dimensions of American politics.

The primary force behind the revolution in campaign attitudes and techniques was a development unforeseen by the men who framed the Constitution—the rise of the party system. Party competition was not at all their original intent. Quite the contrary: inspired at one or two removes by Lord Bolingbroke's British tract of half a century earlier, *The Idea of a Patriot King*, the Founding Fathers envisaged a Patriot President, standing above party and faction, representing the whole people, offering the nation nonpartisan leadership virtuously dedicated to the common good.

The ideal of the Patriot President was endangered, the Founding Fathers believed, by twin menaces—factionalism and factionalism's ugly offspring, the demagogue. Party competition would only encourage unscrupulous men to appeal to popular passion and prejudice. Alexander Hamilton in the 71st Federalist bemoaned the plight of the people, "beset as they continually are . . . by the snares of the ambitious, the avaricious, the desperate, by the artifices of men who possess their confidence more than they deserve it, and of those who seek to possess rather than to deserve it."

Pervading the Federalist was a theme sounded explicitly both in the first paper and the last: the fear that unleashing popular passions would bring on "the military despotism of a victorious demagogue." If the "mischiefs of faction" were, James Madison admitted in the Tenth Federalist, "sown in the nature of man," the object of politics was to repress this insidious disposition, not to yield to it. "If I could not go to heaven but with a party," said Thomas Jefferson, "I would not go there at all."

So the Father of his Country in his Farewell Address solemnly warned his countrymen against "the baneful effects of the spirit of party." That spirit, Washington conceded, was "inseparable from our nature"; but for popular government it was "truly their worst enemy." The "alternate domination of one faction over another," Washington said, would lead in the end to "formal and permanent despotism." The spirit of a party, "a fire not to be quenched . . . demands a uniform vigilance to prevent its bursting into a flame, lest, instead of warming, it should consume."

Yet even as Washington called on Americans to "discourage and restrain" the spirit of party, parties were beginning to crystallize around him. The eruption of partisanship in defiance of such august counsel argued that party competition might well serve functional necessities in the democratic republic.

After all, honest disagreement over policy and principle called for candid debate. And parties, it appeared, had vital roles to play in the consummation of the Constitution. The distribution of powers among three equal branches inclined the national government toward a chronic condition of stalemate. Parties offered the means of overcoming the constitutional separation of powers by coordinating the executive and legislative branches and furnishing the connective tissue essential to effective government. As national associations, moreover, parties were a force against provincialism and separatism. As instruments of compromise, they encouraged, within the parties as well as between them, the containment and mediation of national quarrels, at least until slavery broke the parties up. Henry D. Thoreau cared little enough for politics, but he saw the point: "Politics is, as it were, the gizzard of society, full of grit and gravel, and the two political parties are its two opposite halves, which grind on each other."

Furthermore, as the illustrations in these volumes so gloriously remind us, party competition was a great source of entertainment and fun—all the more important in those faraway days before the advent of baseball and football, of movies and radio and television. "To take a hand in the regulation of society and to discuss it," Alexis de Tocqueville observed when he visited America in the 1830s, "is his biggest concern and, so to speak, the only pleasure an American knows. . . . Even the women frequently attend public meetings and listen to political harangues as a recreation from their household labors. Debating clubs are, to a certain extent, a substitute for theatrical entertainments."

Condemned by the Founding Fathers, unknown to the Constitution, parties nonetheless imperiously forced themselves into political life. But the party system rose from the bottom up. For half a century, the first half-dozen Presidents continued to hold themselves above party. The disappearance of the Federalist Party after the War of 1812 suspended party competition. James Monroe, with no opponent at all in the election of 1820, presided proudly over the Era of Good Feelings, so called because there were no parties around to excite ill feelings. Monroe's successor, John Quincy Adams, despised electioneering and inveighed against the "fashion of peddling for popularity by traveling around the country gathering crowds together, hawking for public dinners, and spouting empty speeches." Men of the old republic believed presidential candidates should be men who already deserved the people's confidence rather than those seeking to win it. Character and virtue, not charisma and ambition, should be the grounds for choosing a President.

Adams was the last of the old school. Andrew Jackson, by beating him in the 1828 election, legitimized party politics and opened a new political era. The rationale of the new school was provided by Jackson's counselor and successor, Martin Van Buren, the classic philosopher of the role of party in the American democracy. By the time Van Buren took his own oath of office in 1837, parties were entrenched as the instruments of American self-government. In Van Buren's words, party battles "rouse the sluggish to exertion, give increased energy to the most active intellect, excite a salutary vigilance over our public functionaries, and prevent that apathy which has proved the ruin of Republics."

Apathy may indeed have proved the ruin of republics, but rousing the sluggish to exertion proved, ironically, the ruin of Van Buren. The architect of the party system became the first casualty of the razzle-dazzle campaigning the system quickly generated. The Whigs' Tippecanoe-and-Tyler-too campaign of 1840 transmuted the democratic Van Buren into a gilded aristocrat and assured his defeat at the polls. The "peddling for popularity" John Quincy Adams had deplored now became standard for party campaigners.

But the new methods were still forbidden to the presidential candidates themselves. The feeling lingered from earlier days that stumping the country in search of votes was demagoguery beneath the dignity of the presidency. Van Buren's code permitted—indeed expected—parties to inscribe their creed in platforms and candidates to declare their principles in letters published in newspapers. Occasionally candidates—William Henry Harrison in 1840, Winfield Scott in 1852—made a speech, but party surrogates did most of the hard work.

As late as 1858, Van Buren, advising his son John, one of the great popular orators of the time, on the best way to make it to the White House, emphasized the "rule . . . that the people will never make a man President who is so importunate as to show by his life and conversation that he not only has an eye on, but is in active pursuit of the office. . . . No man who has laid himself out for it, and was unwise enough to let the people into his secret, ever yet obtained it. Clay, Calhoun, Webster, Scott, and a host of lesser lights, should serve as a guide-post to future aspirants."

The continuing constraint on personal campaigning by candidates was reinforced by the desire of party managers to present their nominees as all things to all men. In 1835 Nicholas Biddle, the wealthy Philadelphian who had been Jackson's mortal opponent in the famous Bank War, advised the Whigs not to let General Harrison "say one single word about his principles or his creed. . . . Let him say nothing, promise nothing. Let no committee, no convention, no town meeting ever extract from him a single word about what he thinks now, or what he will do hereafter. Let the use of pen and ink be wholly forbidden as if he were a mad poet in Bedlam."

We cherish the memory of the famous debates in 1858 between Abraham Lincoln and Stephen A. Douglas. But those debates were not part of a presidential election. When the presidency was at stake two years later, Lincoln gave no campaign speeches on the issues darkly dividing the country. He even expressed doubt about party platforms—"the formal written platform system," as he called it. The candidate's character and record, Lincoln thought, should constitute his platform: "On just such platforms all our earlier and better Presidents were elected."

However, Douglas, Lincoln's leading opponent in 1860, foreshadowed the future when he broke the sound barrier and dared venture forth on thinly disguised campaign tours. Yet Douglas established no immediate precedent. Indeed, half a dozen years later Lincoln's successor, Andrew Johnson, discredited presidential stumping by his "swing around the circle" in the midterm election of 1866. "His performances in a western tour in advocacy of his own election," commented Benjamin F. Butler, who later led the fight in Congress for Johnson's impeachment, ". . . disgusted everybody." The tenth article of impeachment charged Johnson with bringing "the high office of the President of the United States into contempt, ridicule, and disgrace" by delivering "with a loud voice certain intemperate, inflammatory, and scandalous harangues . . . peculiarly indecent and unbecoming in the Chief Magistrate of the United States."

Though presidential candidates Horatio Seymour in 1868, Rutherford B. Hayes in 1876, and James A. Garfield in 1880 made occasional speeches, only Horace Greeley in 1872, James G. Blaine in 1884, and most spectacularly, William Jennings Bryan in 1896 followed Douglas's audacious example of stumping the country. Such tactics continued to provoke disapproval. Bryan, said John Hay, who had been Lincoln's private secretary and was soon to become McKinley's secretary of state, "is begging for the presidency as a tramp might beg for a pie."

Respectable opinion still preferred the "front porch" campaign, employed by Garfield, by Benjamin Harrison in 1888, and most notably by McKinley in 1896. Here candidates received and addressed numerous delegations at their own homes—a form, as the historian Gil Troy writes, of "stumping in place."

While candidates generally continued to stand on their dignity, popular campaigning in presidential elections flourished in these years, attaining new heights of participation (82 percent of eligible voters in 1876 and never once from 1860 to 1900 under 70 percent) and new wonders of pyrotechnics and ballyhoo. Parties mobilized the electorate as never before, and political iconography was never more ingenious and fantastic. "Politics, considered not as the science of government, but as the art of winning elections and securing office," wrote the keen British observer James Bryce, "has reached in the United States a development surpassing in elaborateness that of England or France as much as the methods of those countries surpass the methods of

Servia or Roumania." Bryce marveled at the "military discipline" of the parties, at "the demonstrations, the parades and receptions, the badges and brass bands and triumphal arches," at the excitement stirred by elections— and at "the disproportion that strikes a European between the merits of the presidential candidate and the blazing enthusiasm which he evokes."

Still the old taboo held back the presidential candidates themselves. Even so irrepressible a campaigner as President Theodore Roosevelt felt obliged to hold his tongue when he ran for reelection in 1904. This unwonted abstinence reminded him, he wrote in considerable frustration, of the July day in 1898 when he was "lying still under shell fire" during the Spanish-American War. "I have continually wished that I could be on the stump myself."

No such constraint inhibited TR, however, when he ran again for the presidency in 1912. Meanwhile, and for the first time, *both* candidates in 1908—Bryan again, and William Howard Taft—actively campaigned for the prize. The duties of the office, on top of the new requirements of campaigning, led Woodrow Wilson to reflect that same year, four years before he himself ran for President, "Men of ordinary physique and discretion cannot be Presidents and live, if the strain be not somehow relieved. We shall be obliged always to be picking our chief magistrates from among wise and prudent athletes,—a small class."

Theodore Roosevelt and Woodrow Wilson combined to legitimate a new conception of presidential candidates as active molders of public opinion in active pursuit of the highest office. Once in the White House, Wilson revived the custom, abandoned by Jefferson, of delivering annual state of the union addresses to Congress in person. In 1916 he became the first incumbent President to stump for his own reelection.

The activist candidate and the bully-pulpit presidency were expressions of the growing democratization of politics. New forms of communication were reconfiguring presidential campaigns. In the nineteenth century the press, far more fiercely partisan then than today, had been the main carrier of political information. In the twentieth century the spread of advertising techniques and the rise of the electronic media—radio, television, computerized public opinion polling—wrought drastic changes in the methodology of politics. In particular the electronic age diminished and now threatens to dissolve the historic role of the party.

The old system had three tiers: the politician at one end; the voter at the other; and the party in between. The party's function was to negotiate between the politician and the voters, interpreting each to the other and providing the link that held the political process together. The electric revolution has substantially abolished the sovereignty of the party. Where once the voter turned to the local party leader to find out whom to support, now he looks at television and makes up his own mind. Where once the politician turned to the local party leader to find out what people are thinking, he now takes a computerized poll.

The electronic era has created a new breed of professional consultants, "handlers," who by the 1980s had taken control of campaigns away from the politicians. The traditional pageantry—rallies, torchlight processions, volunteers, leaflets, billboards, bumper stickers—is now largely a thing of the past. Television replaces the party as the means of mobilizing the voter. And as the party is left to wither on the vine, the presidential candidate becomes more pivotal than ever. We shall see the rise of personalist movements, founded not on historic organizations but on compelling personalities, private fortunes, and popular frustrations. Without the stabilizing influence of parties, American politics would grow angrier, wilder, and more irresponsible.

Things have changed considerably from the austerities of the old republic. Where once voters preferred to call presumably reluctant candidates to the duties of the supreme magistracy and rejected pursuit of the office as evidence of dangerous ambition, now they expect candidates to come to them, explain their views and plead for their support. Where nonpartisan virtue had been the essence, now candidates must prove to voters that they have the requisite "fire in the belly." "'Twud be inth'restin," said Mr. Dooley, ". . . if th' fathers iv th' counthry cud come back an' see what has happened while they've been away. In times past whin ye voted f'r prisident ye didn't vote f'r a man. Ye voted f'r a kind iv a statue that ye'd put up in ye'er own mind on a marble pidistal. Ye nivir heerd iv George Wash'nton goin' around th' counthry distributin' five cint see-gars."

We have reversed the original notion that ambition must be disguised and the office seek the man. Now the man—and soon, one must hope, the woman— seeks the office and does so without guilt or shame or inhibition. This is not necessarily a degradation of democracy. Dropping the disguise is a gain for candor, and personal avowals of convictions and policies may elevate and educate the electorate.

On the other hand, the electronic era has dismally reduced both the intellectual content of campaigns and the attention span of audiences. In the nineteenth century political speeches lasted for a couple of hours and dealt with issues in systematic and exhaustive fashion. Voters drove wagons for miles to hear Webster and Clay, Bryan and Teddy Roosevelt, and felt cheated if the famous orator did not give them their money's worth. Then radio came along and cut political addresses down first to an hour, soon to thirty minutes—still enough time to develop substantive arguments.

But television has shrunk the political talk first to fifteen minutes, now to the sound bite and the thirty-second spot. Advertising agencies today sell candidates with all the cynical contrivance they previously devoted to selling detergents and mouthwash. The result is the debasement of American politics. "The idea that you can merchandise candidates for high office like breakfast cereal," Adlai Stevenson said in 1952, "is the ultimate indignity to the democratic process."

Still Bryce's "intermittent fever" will be upon us every fourth year. We will continue to watch wise if not always prudent athletes in their sprint for the White House, enjoy the quadrennial spectacle and agonize about the outcome.

"The strife of the election," said Lincoln after his reelection in 1864, "is but human-nature practically applied to the facts. What has occurred in this case, must ever recur in similar cases. Human-nature will not change."

Lincoln, as usual, was right. Despite the transformation in political methods there remains a basic continuity in political emotions. "For a long while before the appointed time has come," Tocqueville wrote more than a century and a half ago, "the election becomes the important and, so to speak, the all-engrossing topic of discussion. Factional ardor is redoubled, and all the artificial passions which the imagination can create in a happy and peaceful land are agitated and brought to light. . . .

"As the election draws near, the activity of intrigue and the agitation of the populace increase; the citizens are divided into hostile camps, each of which assumes the name of its favorite candidate; the whole nation glows with feverish excitement; the election is the daily theme of the press, the subject of every private conversation, the end of every thought and every action, the sole interest of the present.

"It is true," Tocqueville added, "that as soon as the choice is determined, this ardor is dispelled, calm returns, and the river, which had nearly broken its banks, sinks to its usual level; but who can refrain from astonishment that such a storm should have arisen?"

The election storm in the end blows fresh and clean. With the tragic exception of 1860, the American people have invariably accepted the result and given the victor their hopes and blessings. For all its flaws and follies, democracy abides.

Let us now turn the pages and watch the gaudy parade of American presidential politics pass by in all its careless glory.

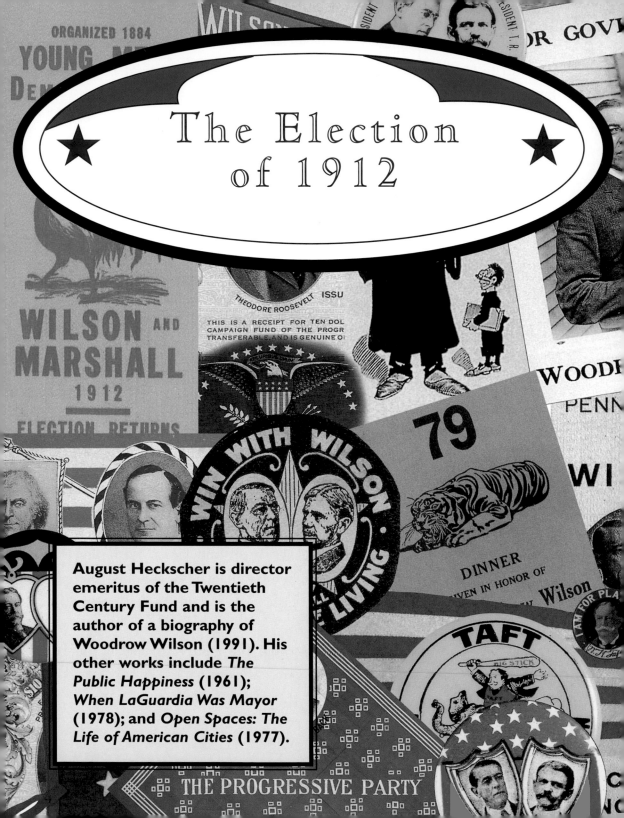

The Election of 1912

August Heckscher is director emeritus of the Twentieth Century Fund and is the author of a biography of Woodrow Wilson (1991). His other works include *The Public Happiness* (1961); *When LaGuardia Was Mayor* (1978); and *Open Spaces: The Life of American Cities* (1977).

The campaign of 1912 was to be the stage for a great debate between the two towering political figures of the time—Theodore Roosevelt and Woodrow Wilson. It was to be the stage where the form and spirit of progressivism were defined. Not least, it was to be the arena where many of the techniques of modern political campaigning revealed themselves. All this came about through such mysterious and unanticipated events as make the study of American politics endlessly absorbing.

Four years earlier the Roosevelt-Wilson confrontation was as remote a possibility as might have been readily conceived. After two terms in the White House Roosevelt in 1908 renounced the opportunity to run again, making William Howard Taft, his handpicked candidate and close friend, his successor. Wilson was still president of Princeton University. That Wilson would become a spectacularly successful governor of New Jersey, and that Roosevelt would come to a bitter break with Taft, defied prophecy.

By the spring of 1912 Wilson had emerged as an intriguing national figure, but by no means an obvious choice of the national nominating convention. At Baltimore his chief rival, Champ Clark, gained a majority of the votes; then in frenzied scenes Wilson climbed, ballot by suspenseful ballot, until on the forty-sixth roll call he gained the two-thirds majority required for the nomination. The Republicans' choice of Taft a week earlier had played a major role in making it seem expedient to Democratic strategists that they name their most dynamic and liberal candidate. The choice of Taft had also stimulated Roosevelt to enter the race as the nominee of the soon-to-be formed Progressive Party.

The Democratic convention had been turbulent, with popular opinion making itself felt at every turn. Pro-Wilson crowds in the galleries

A selection of items from the 1908 campaign. The election of 1908 was the last of William Jennings Bryan's three presidential races. His defeat forced the Democratic Party to search for new leaders. Among Republicans, power shifted from Theodore Roosevelt to William Howard Taft and foreshadowed the divisive split the party would suffer in 1912.

A DEMOCRAT

Is a Man who has voted for William Jennings Bryan twice, and is now Ready to do so again.

In these political postcards from the 1908 election, Bryan is associated with Thomas Jefferson and Andrew Jackson, and Taft with Roosevelt.

played almost as important a role—and made almost as much noise—as delegates on the floor. As with the nomination of Wendell Willkie a generation later, telegrams from an aroused and sympathetic public arrived by the thousands, the overwhelming majority in favor of the apparent underdog and outsider. The direct impact of the populace, embodied in the new presidential primaries, carried over into the convention, and played a part in Wilson's nomination.

The Chicago convention, which met in August to found the Progressive Party and to anoint Roosevelt as its candidate, also provided wild scenes but with a different and unique character. It took its tone in part from the Roosevelt saga—the tradition of big-game hunting and of the Rough Riders—and in part from religious fervor. Roosevelt may have ached to battle like a Bull Moose, but most of his followers were more inclined to sing "Onward Christian Soldiers." The candidate bridged the gap (at least temporarily) by making his address to the convention a "Confession of

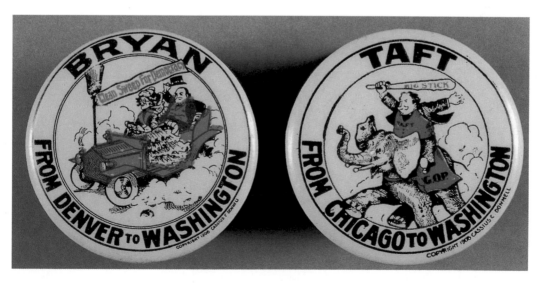

Pair of 1908 caricature buttons showing Bryan and Taft traveling from their respective convention cities to the White House.

FOR GOVERNOR

WOODROW WILSON

Woodrow Wilson was elected governor of New Jersey in 1910. A political scientist and lawyer, he was the first nonclerical president of Princeton University (1902–1910).

Faith." A stirring appeal to the progressive spirit, it struck the characteristically Rooseveltian note of heroic and self-sacrificing leadership.

In the following three-cornered campaign (the nomination of Eugene V. Debs by the Socialist Party was not at the time considered politically important) the Republican candidate quickly faded from view. Taft had disliked being President; he referred to his administration as "humdrum" and in private letters wondered why anyone should want to vote for him. His wife was ailing; Archie Butt, his trusted confidante, had recently died; and the break with Roosevelt both saddened and embittered him. An unreconstructed conservative, Taft found himself out of tune with the people's mood. He did not campaign actively, and the immense advantage of being an incumbent he was unable to make count, being both inept politically and generally unpopular. He delivered an acceptance address and then withdrew from active campaigning. The field was left to Roosevelt and Wilson, as the fates no doubt had intended all along that it should be.

The debate between these two charismatic figures was slow in finding its central theme. Before starting on the campaign trail, Roosevelt had to get his new party organized. Wilson had a number of political chores to put

Postcard circa 1911–1912. Strife in Republican ranks broke into open warfare in 1910. Beginning in August, Roosevelt publicized his differences with President Taft. Some Republican clubs urged that Roosevelt receive the 1912 Republican nomination.

out of the way. The problem of a campaign manager was particularly sensitive. The temperamental and ailing William F. McCombs had been his manager at Baltimore, yet seemed a poor choice for the larger challenge. Fearful of being charged with ingratitude, Wilson reluctantly stood by McCombs. The candidate also had scores to settle with the New York and New Jersey bosses, and a party to heal after the disruptions of Baltimore. Lingering at Sea Girt, the official residence of New Jersey governors, Wilson received delegations, delivered his acceptance address (in those days it was still the custom to await formal notification by messengers that might as well have come on horseback), and cleared his mind with regard to campaign issues.

In his primary campaigns Wilson had talked frequently about the trusts, but his policy in regard to them remained vague. In general he favored a legalistic approach, defining abuses and holding individuals responsible for misconduct. This seemed a

Representatives of the Democratic National Committee officially informed Wilson that the convention had nominated him for president. This notification ceremony took place at Wilson's Sea Girt, New Jersey, home on August 7, 1912.

pale remedy in comparison to the outright policing of big business long advocated by Roosevelt. A meeting with the noted liberal lawyer, Louis D. Brandeis, late in September at Sea Girt, changed all this. Brandeis expounded to Wilson the concepts of a regulated market, one that would ensure competition even among large organizations. From Wilson's point of view this had the immense advantage of eliminating the necessity for a powerful government commission—of big government set up as a counterweight to big business. To establish by political intervention the conditions of a free market, and then to let business compete within that market, seemed to him the solution in accord with all his political predispositions. At Buffalo three days later, in an effective speech which opened his campaign, Wilson showed how much he had profited from the meeting with Brandeis.

This revised approach to the trusts issue formed the basis of Wilson's New Freedom; as Roosevelt's approach formed the basis of the New Nationalism. Between these two neatly packaged slogans, encompassing two opposed and meaningful concepts, the lines of the great argument were drawn. As that argument was spun out in campaign addresses, the vision of the two candidates went well beyond the issue of the trusts. The New Nationalism was set in relation to Roosevelt's whole approach to government, with its vigorous, unembarrassed use of power to achieve social as well as economic justice. The New Freedom

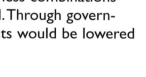

Paper sticker supporting Wilson and Marshall. Wilson believed that business combinations had become too powerful. Through government regulation, living costs would be lowered for average Americans.

Roosevelt and Johnson

VOTE THE FULL **ROOSEVELT**

BULL MOOSE TICKET

THE ONLY REAL ROOSEVELT TICKET IN LANCASTER COUNTY

"*For there is neither East nor West,
Border nor Breed nor Birth,
When two strong men stand face to face
Though they come from the ends of the earth.*"
—Kipling

Items from the 1912 Progressive (Bull Moose) campaign. Left: Poster of Roosevelt and Johnson with stirring Kipling quotation. Below left: paper certificate given for a $10 party contribution. Below right: Roosevelt campaign buttons.

1912 Progressive Party cotton bandanna with legend "We Want Our Teddy Back/Born in 1912." The Progressive Party was nicknamed the Bull Moose Party after one of Roosevelt's favorite sayings: "I am as strong as a bull moose."

THE PROGRESSIVE PARTY

became related to Wilson's ideal of a social order where the emphasis was upon those in the midst of the battle, men on the make, struggling towards the light; and where the aim of politics was to give them a fair field and mitigation of the worst of industrial ills.

In setting forth their disparate messages each candidate had his own style. Roosevelt's was abrupt, staccato, often shrill. He was not an orator in any traditional sense—Wilson he derided for his "empty locution." He cared little about wooing his audiences, rather taking them by assault and startling them into recognition. He admitted to a "certain lack of sequitur that I do not seem able to get rid of." Yet his phrases, often clichés, stuck in the mind and seemed to be the essence of the man. "I try to put the whole truth in one sentence," he explained; again: "find the phrases the newspapers will quote, and you can get your message across."

In this way Roosevelt was getting very close to the "sound bite" of today's television; with him, one recent scholar asserts, "we stand at the edge of the advertised politics of the late twentieth century."

Wilson's way of imparting his message was very different. From youth he had trained himself in the art of public speaking. He, too, despised oratory—the bombast of the spellbinder or the harangue from the stump. He cultivated the style of the great parliamentarians, conversational in tone, free of gestures, and addressed directly, it appeared, to each individual in his audience. His words—spoken extemporaneously (his speeches, he told reporters, "come right out of my mind as it is working at the time")—flowed seamlessly from a bottomless reserve, moving from the simplest discourse to highly colored, imaginative flights.

In the campaign of 1912 he dealt in simple terms with the more technical aspects of the tariff or the trusts: "My dream of politics, all my life," he said, "has been that it is the common business, that it is something we owe to each other to understand." But this did not preclude passages of striking eloquence. Of William Pitt he had written when still a student at Princeton that his "imagination was powerful enough to invest all plans of national policy with a poetic charm." The later Wilson was not devoid of this gift.

To reach the public they hoped to persuade the candidates were put to tests that even Roosevelt, the Bull Moose, was not always up to. After the summer of preparation the two crisscrossed the country by train, making three or four major speeches a day, often an hour or more in length, in conditions that seemed designed to defeat all attempts at rational discussion. They spoke in ball

Group of celluloid buttons issued by the 1912 Progressive Party. Roosevelt's followers used "Onward Christian Soldiers" as their campaign song and acted as crusaders in a national religious revival.

parks, on race tracks, at country fairs; in opera houses, in huge convention halls, sometimes before audiences as large as thirty thousand—all this without any means of amplifying the human voice.

Once back on the train, they found that a schedule of frequent stops brought more calls for speeches. Particularly disliking these rear platform appearances, Wilson demurred good humoredly. "This is the kind of platform that I don't like to stand on," he advised one awaiting crowd. "It moves around and shifts its ground too often. I like a platform that stays put." Then he would embark on an argu-

Novelty postcards with springs for tails. These were sold during the 1912 campaign. A symbol of Roosevelt's Progressive Party was the bull moose.

Of Course I'm For

WILSON

After Careful Thought

I'm Going Home to Vote for

ROOSEVELT

If it Takes 'till November

ONLY 900 MILES TO GO

By Gum

TAFT

Will Do For Me

Set of pennant theme postcards.

ment, and as often as not be cut short when the train whistled and started off.

Roosevelt's simplified, appealing and bombastic speaking style seemed to get across better in such conditions. But Roosevelt was troubled by the kind of audiences he was drawing and by some of the manifestations of their enthusiasm. He had declared himself ready to stand at Armageddon and to battle for the Lord; but he was at bottom the self-disciplined patrician who mistrusted emotionalism and extremists of any kind. He had spoken of the "lunatic fringe" that surrounds efforts at reform; he had taken from Bunyan the epithet "muckraker" for those who saw more political corruption than he was prepared to take account of. Later he would look back upon the Progressive Party as a home for the "cranks" of his day. The fevered demonstrations that greeted him, the hymn-singing, the display of bandannas, cowboy hats, banners, and campaign buttons was disconcerting to one who, for all his flamboyance, was trying to speak seriously to the people.

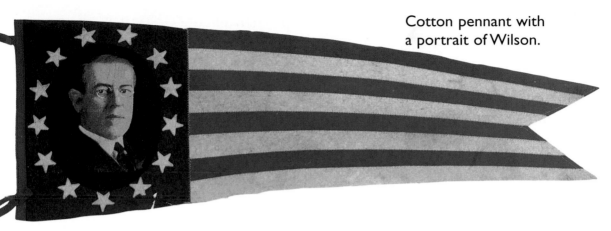

Cotton pennant with a portrait of Wilson.

In Roosevelt's advocacy of the New Nationalism there was more than a touch of Alexander Hamilton. Wilson, by contrast, wore the mantle of Jeffersonianism. The New Freedom was constructed on belief in the common man, and the candidate himself, in his patient, low-keyed approach to campaigning, in his emphasis upon lucid argument and rational appeals, bore something of the earlier Democrat's stamp. But Wilson's message, like that of his adversary, was almost drowned out by the fervor of the mass audiences. He had difficulty in making himself heard; he was in competition with brass bands and unruly demonstrators; he suffered from faulty acoustics in the halls where he spoke.

In an early speech, arguing in favor of the common man's ascendancy, Wilson let slip the assertion that "the history of liberty is a history of the limitation of governmental power, not the increase of it." Roosevelt saw this as proof that Wilson was not the progressive he pretended to be; in speech after speech he denounced what he considered an academic reversion to *laissez-faire*. Having found his issue, Roosevelt pounded upon it mercilessly. Repetition became a technique that later presidential campaigners would also used to their advantage. Yet if his charge was misleading and based upon a sentence taken out of contest, it was not a fair sample of the campaign as a whole, which was singularly free from personal attacks or unfair innuendoes.

Toward his rival Wilson adopted an attitude of jaunty defiance. The Bull Moose Party was made up of "the irregular Republicans, the variegated Republicans," he said in one campaign speech; Roosevelt would, if elected, be a lonely man, but perhaps that did not matter since "he finds himself rather good company." Roosevelt was not moved by the extreme personal animosity he later felt toward Wilson. He was an able man, he wrote privately at the time, who would probably serve creditably if elected; indeed Roosevelt expressed some doubt as to whether he should be running against him. It was as if he had a certain fascination with this new type of adversary. "It was Wilson, Wilson, Wilson all the time in the private car," recalled one of Roosevelt's press aides.

By mid-October both candidates were feeling the strain of the long debate. Roosevelt's voice, never robust, was beginning to fail; Wilson referred to his own "impaired voice"—impaired, he told one crowd, "in your service." Both men needed a rest, and on October 14 the event occurred that dramatically changed the course of the campaign. Outside his hotel in Milwaukee, on his way to deliver a speech at the municipal auditorium, Roosevelt was shot by a fanatic; he narrowly escaped death, the bullet being deflected by his eyeglass case and the bulky manuscript of his speech. Roosevelt spent the next ten days in a hospital; Wilson, in Princeton, waited out his opponent's recovery.

Roosevelt's bravura performance immediately after the shooting underscored his innate bravery and the almost mythic quality of his leadership. He asked that his assailant be treated without violence; then he proceeded to the auditorium where he spoke to a hushed audience. "Friends," he began, "I shall have to ask you to be as quiet as possible . . . I have been shot . . . the bullet is in me now [showing the location of the wound] so that I cannot make a very long speech . . . I can tell you with absolute truthfulness," he continued, "that I am very much uninterested in whether I am shot or not." His speech lasted more than an hour, mixing

Wilson postcard using rowboat motif for "Wood-Row" wordplay. Roosevelt struggles to catch up to a relaxed Wilson in the race to the White House. Taft flails behind.

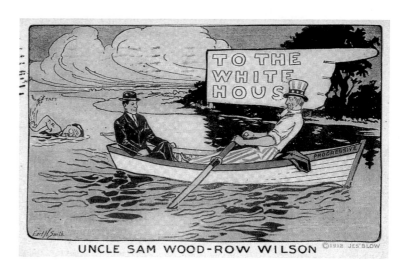

UNCLE SAM WOOD-ROW WILSON

familiar themes with exalted appeals for heroism.

It was questioned whether the shooting might not create a large sympathy vote for Roosevelt. But by then Wilson was clearly leading in the three-cornered race, and it was only left to close down the campaign with the customary ritual of mass rallies in the East, especially at the Madison Square Garden in New York. On the climactic occasion Wilson was cheered for seventy minutes, more than twenty minutes longer than Roosevelt had been on his dramatic reappearance the previous night. Clearly moved, Wilson said afterwards he forgot what he had planned to say, but he managed well enough to please the crowd, and victory was in the air.

The results, when they became known, showed Wilson to have a sweeping electoral victory—435 votes with only 88 for Roosevelt and 8 (Vermont and Utah) for the hapless Taft. But the popular vote told a different story. Wilson failed to get a majority, polling fewer votes than Roosevelt and Taft together. For reasons still obscure, after a campaign devoted mostly to invocations of Marx and praise of socialism, Debs polled nearly a million votes. Roosevelt retired to lick his wounds, and Wilson toiled for another four years before a remarkable personal victory gave him the popular majority that had eluded him in 1912.

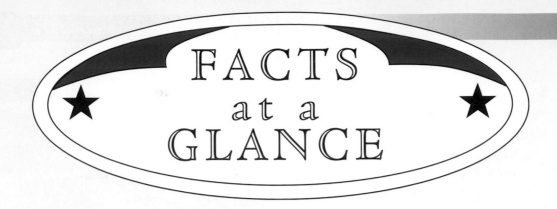

WOODROW WILSON

- **Born:** December 28, 1856, in Staunton, Virginia
- **Parents:** Joseph and Jessie Janet Woodrow Wilson
- **Education:** graduated from the College of New Jersey (Princeton University) in 1879
- **Occupation:** teacher, administrator, public official
- **Married:** Ellen Louise Axson (1860–1914) on June 24, 1885; Edith Bolling Galt (1872–1961) on December 18, 1915.
- **Children:** Margaret Woodrow Wilson (1886–1944); Jesse Woodrow Wilson (1887–1933); Eleanor Randolph Wilson (1889–1967).
- **Died:** February 3, 1924, in Washington, D.C.

Served as the 28th PRESIDENT OF THE UNITED STATES,

- March 4, 1913, to March 3, 1921

VICE PRESIDENT

- Thomas R. Marshall, 1913–1921

OTHER POLITICAL POSITIONS

- Governor of New Jersey, 1911–1913

CABINET

Secretary of State

- William J. Bryan (1913–15)
- Robert Lansing (1915–20)
- Bainbridge Colby (1920–21)

Secretary of the Treasury

- William G. McAdoo (1913–18)
- Carter Glass (1918–20)
- David F. Houston (1920–21)

Secretary of War

- Lindley M. Garrison (1913–16)
- Newton D. Baker (1916–21)

Attorney General

- James C. McReynolds (1913–14)
- Thomas W. Gregory (1914–19)
- A. Mitchell Palmer (1919–21)

Postmaster General

- Albert S. Burleson (1913–21)

Secretary of the Navy

- Josephus Daniels (1913–21)

Secretary of the Interior

- Franklin K. Lane (1913–20)
- John B. Payne (1920–21)

Secretary of Agriculture

- David F. Houston (1913–20)
- Edwin T. Meredith (1920–21)

Secretary of Commerce

- William C. Redfield (1913–19)
- Joshua W. Alexander (1919–21)

Secretary of Labor

- William B. Wilson (1913–21)

NOTABLE EVENTS DURING WILSON'S ADMINISTRATION

1913   Woodrow Wilson is sworn in as the 28th president of the United States on March 4.

1914   Wilson proclaims U.S. neutrality in the war in Europe; the Panama Canal is officially opened August 15.

1915   The British ship *Lusitania* is sunk on May 7 by a German submarine, killing 128 American passengers; Wilson protests to Germany; U.S. troops land in Haiti on July 28, and the island nation becomes a U. S. protectorate September 16.

1916   American troops under General John Pershing pursue Francisco "Pancho" Villa over the Mexican border. Villa sought to regain Mexican lands that had been ceded to the United States.

1917   The United States cuts diplomatic ties with Germany after that nation declares unrestricted submarine warfare on January 31; U.S. formally declares war on Germany on April 6, 1917.

1918   The Sedition Amendment is added to the Espionage Act, making it illegal to speak out against the war or criticize the government; Wilson gives Fourteen Points speech, outlining American war goals; World War I ends on November 11.

1919   Treaty of Versailles signed on June 28; the Eighteenth Amendment is ratified, ushering in the Prohibition period.

1920   The Senate rejects United States membership in the League of Nations, weakening that international body; the Nineteenth Amendment, which gives women the right to vote, is ratified.

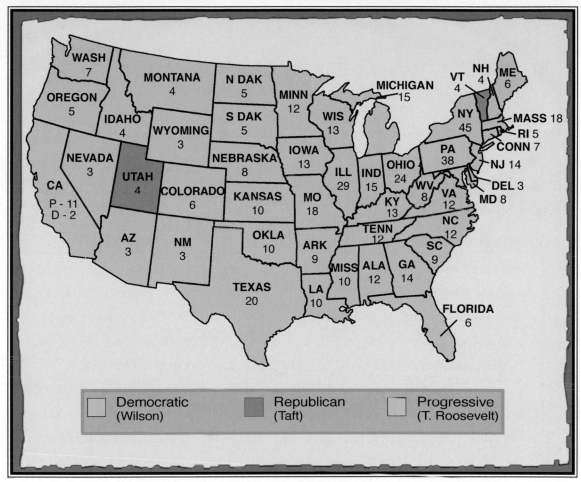

| Democratic (Wilson) | Republican (Taft) | Progressive (T. Roosevelt) |

Woodrow Wilson, the Democratic candidate, benefited from a split in the Republican Party. Wilson won an easy victory in the electoral college, receiving 435 votes to 88 for Progressive Party candidate Theodore Roosevelt and just eight votes for incumbent president William Howard Taft, the Republican candidate. Nationally, Wilson received a plurality of the vote, winning nearly 6.3 million (41.8 percent) while Roosevelt won 4.1 million (27.4 percent) and Taft nearly 3.5 million (23.2 percent). Eugene V. Debs, the Socialist Party candidate running for the fourth time, made his strongest showing to that point. Although he did not receive any electoral votes, Debs won about 900,000 votes, 6 percent of the total.

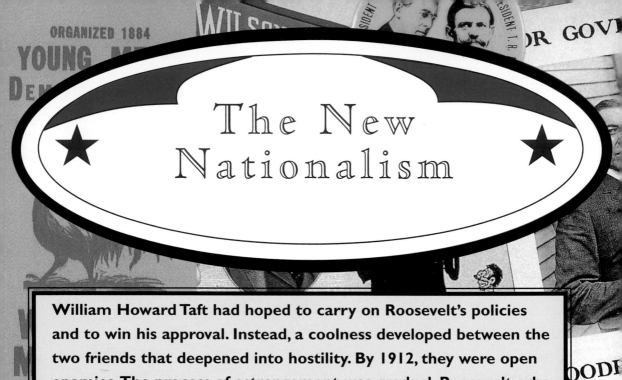

The New Nationalism

William Howard Taft had hoped to carry on Roosevelt's policies and to win his approval. Instead, a coolness developed between the two friends that deepened into hostility. By 1912, they were open enemies. The process of estrangement was gradual. Roosevelt, who returned from an African hunting trip and a triumphal tour through Europe in June 1910, had avoided open criticism of his hand-picked successor. However, in several speeches, he enunciated his new creed, called the New Nationalism. "I stand for a square deal," he said. "But I mean not merely that I stand for fair play under the present rules of the game, but that I stand for having those rules changed so as to work for a more substantial equality of opportunity and reward." This new Roosevelt approach to social problems meant the abandonment of *laissez faire* and the assumption by the federal government of additional responsibilities.

In late summer 1910, Roosevelt began a speaking tour in the West. On August 31, at Osawatomie, Kansas, he declared that "property shall be the servant and not the master," and that the Constitution, if too rigid to conform to the needs of life, must be amended. This speech, excerpted here, is considered Roosevelt's clearest explanation of the New Nationalism.

We come here today to commemorate one of the epochmaking events of the long struggle for the rights of man—the long struggle for the uplift of humanity. Our country—this great Republic—means nothing unless it means the triumph of a real democracy, the triumph of popular government, and, in the long run, of an economic system under which each man shall be guaranteed the opportunity to show the best that there is in him. That is why the history of America is now the central feature of the history of the world; for the world has set its face hopefully toward our democracy; and, O my fellow citizens, each one of you carries on your shoulders not only the burden of doing well for the sake of your own country, but the burden of doing well and of seeing that this nation does well for the sake of mankind. [. . .]

Practical equality of opportunity for all citizens, when we achieve it, will have two great results. First, every man will have a fair chance to make of himself all that in him lies; to reach the highest point to which his capacities, unassisted by special privilege of his own and unhampered by the special privilege of others, can carry him, and to get for himself and his family substantially what he has earned. Second, equality of opportunity means that the commonwealth will get from every citizen the highest service of which he is capable. No man who carries the burden of the special privileges of another can give to the commonwealth that service to which it is fairly entitled.

I stand for the square deal. But when I say that I am for the square deal, I mean not merely that I stand for fair play under the present rules of the games, but that I stand for having those rules changed so as to work for a more substantial equality of opportunity and of reward for equally good service. [. . .]

Now, this means that our government, national and State, must be freed from the sinister influence or control of special interests. [. . .] We must drive the special interests out of politics. That is one of our tasks today. Every special interest is entitled to justice—full, fair, and complete—and, now, mind you, if there were any attempt by mob-violence to plunder and work harm to the special interest, whatever it may be, and I most dislike and the wealthy man, whomsoever he may be, for whom I have the greatest contempt, I would fight for him, and you would if you were worth your salt. He should have justice. For every special interest is entitled to justice, but not one is entitled to a vote in Congress, to a voice on the bench, or to representation in any public office. The Constitution guarantees protections to property, and we must make that promise good. But it does not give the right of suffrage to any corporation.

The true friend of property, the true conservative, is he who insists that property shall be the servant and not the master of the commonwealth; who insists that the creature of man's making shall be the servant and not the master of the man who made it. The citizens of the United States must effectively control the mighty commercial forces which they have themselves called into being. There can be no effective control of corporations while their political activity remains. To put an end to it will be neither a short nor an easy task, but it can be done.

We must have complete and effective publicity of corporate affairs, so that people may know beyond peradventure whether the corporations obey the law and whether their management entitles them to the confidence of the public. It is necessary that laws should be passed to prohibit the use of corporate funds directly or indirectly for political purposes; it is still more necessary that such laws should be thoroughly enforced. Corporate expenditures for political purposes, and especially such expenditures by public-service corporations, have supplied one of the principal sources of corruption in our political affairs.

It has become entirely clear that we must have government supervision of the capitalization, not only of public-service corporations, including, particularly, railways, but of all corporations doing an interstate business. I do not

Silk bandanna with symbols reflecting Roosevelt's extraordinary charisma—bull moose, bear, big stick, toothy smile, spectacles, hat in the ring.

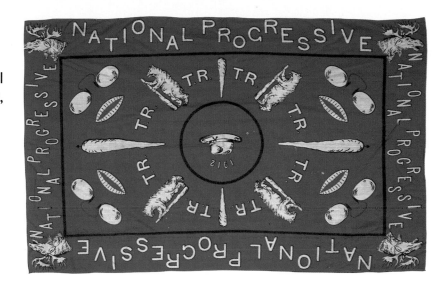

wish to see the nation forced into the ownership of the railways if it can possibly be avoided, and the only alternative is thoroughgoing and effective regulation, which shall be based on a full knowledge of all the facts, including a physical valuation of property. [. . .]

I believe the officers, and, especially, the directors, of corporations should be held personally responsible when any corporation breaks the law. [. . .]

There is a wide-spread belief among our people that under the methods of making tariffs, which have hitherto obtained, the special interests are too influential. Probably this is true of both the big special interests and the little special interests. These methods have put a premium on selfishness, and, naturally, the selfish big interests have gotten more than their smaller, though equally selfish brothers. The duty of Congress is to provide a method by which the interest of the whole people shall be all that receives consideration. To this end there must be an expert tariff commission, wholly removed from the possibility of political pressure or of improper business influence. Such a commission can find the real difference between cost of production, which is mainly the difference of labor cost here and abroad. As fast as its recommendations are made, I believe in revising one schedule at a time. A general revision of the tariff almost inevitably leads to logrolling and the subordination of the general public interest to local and special interests.

The absence of effective State, and, especially, national, restraint upon unfair money-getting has tended to create a small class of enormously wealthy and economically powerful men, whose chief object is to hold and increase their power. The prime need is to change the conditions which enable these men to accumulate power which is not for the general welfare that they should hold or exercise. We grudge no man a fortune which represents his own power and sagacity, when exercised with entire regard to the welfare of his fellows. Again, comrades over there, take the lesson from your own experience. Not only did you not grudge, but you gloried in the promotion of the great generals who gained their promotion by leading the army to victory. So it is with us. We grudge no man a fortune in civil life if it is honorably obtained and well used. It is not even enough that it should have gained without doing damage to the community. We should permit it to be gained only so long as the gaining represents benefit to the community. This, I know, implies a policy of a far more active governmental interference with social and economic conditions in this country than we have yet had, but I think we have got to face the fact that such an increase in governmental control is now necessary.

No man should receive a dollar unless that dollar has been fairly earned. Every dollar received should represent a dollar's worth of service rendered— not gambling in stocks, but service rendered. The really big fortune, the swollen fortune, by the mere fact of its size acquires qualities which differentiate it in kind as well as in degree from what is possessed by men of relatively small means. Therefore, I believe in a graduated income tax on big fortunes, and in another tax which is far more easily collected and far more effective—a graduated inheritance tax on big fortunes, properly safeguarded against evasion and increasing rapidly in amount with the size of the estate.

The people of the United States suffer from periodical financial panics to a degree substantially unknown among the other nations which approach us in financial strength. There is no reason why we should suffer what they escape. It is of profound importance that our financial system should be promptly investigated, and so thoroughly and effectively revised as to make it certain that hereafter our currency will no longer fail at critical times to meet our needs. [. . .]

Nothing is more true than that excess of every kind is followed by reaction; a fact which should be pondered by reformer and reactionary alike. We are face to face with new conceptions of the relations of property to human welfare, chiefly because certain advocates of the rights of property as against the rights of men have been pushing their claims too far. The man who wrongly holds that every human right is secondary to his profit must now give way to the advocate of human welfare, who rightly maintains that every man holds his property subject to the general right of the community to regulate its use to whatever degree the public welfare may require it.

But I think we may go still further. The right to regulate the use of wealth in the public interest is universally admitted. Let us admit also the right to regulate the terms and conditions of labor, which is the chief element of wealth, directly in the interest of the common good. The fundamental thing to do for every man is to give him a chance to reach a place in which he will make the greatest possible contribution to the public welfare. Understand what I say there. Give him a chance, not push him up if he will not be pushed. Help any man who stumbles; if he lies down, it is a poor job to try to carry him; but if he is a worthy man, try your best to see that he gets a chance to show the worth that is in him.

No man can be a good citizen unless he has a wage more than sufficient to cover the bare cost of living, and hours of labor short enough so that after his day's work is done he will have time and energy to bear his share in the management of the community, to help in carrying the general load. We keep countless men from being good citizens by the conditions of life with which we surround them. We need comprehensive workmen's compensation acts, both State and national laws to regulate child labor and work for women, and, especially, we need in our common schools not merely education in booklearning, but also practical training for daily life and work. We need to enforce better sanitary conditions for our workers and to extend the use of safety appliances for our workers in industry and commerce, both within and between the States. Also, friends, in the interest of the working man himself we need to set our faces like Mint against mob-violence just as against corporate greed; against violence and injustice and lawlessness by wage-workers just as much as against lawless cunning and greed and selfish arrogance of employers.

If I could ask but one thing of my fellow countrymen, my request would be that, whenever they go in for reform, they remember the two sides, and that they always exact justice from one side as much as from the other. I have small use for the public servant who can always see and denounce the corruption of the capitalist, but who cannot persuade himself, especially before elections, to say a word about lawless mob-violence. And I have equally small use for the man, be he a judge on the bench, or editor of a great paper, or wealthy and influential private citizen, who can see clearly enough and denounce the lawlessness of mob-violence, but whose eyes are closed so that he is blind when the question is one of corruption in business on a gigantic scale. [. . .]

The American people are right in demanding that New Nationalism, without which we cannot hope to deal with new problems. The New Nationalism puts the national need before sectional or personal advantage. It is impatient of the utter confusion that results from local legislatures attempting to treat national issues as local issues. It is still more impatient of the impotence which springs from overdivision of governmental powers, the impotence which makes it possible for local selfishness or for legal cunning, hired by wealthy special interests, to bring national activities to a deadlock. This New Nationalism regards the executive power as the steward of the public welfare. It demands of the judiciary that it shall be interested primarily in human welfare rather than in property, just as it demands that the representative body shall represent all the people rather than any one class or section of the people. [. . .]

If our political institutions were perfect, they would absolutely prevent the political domination of money in any part of our affairs. We need to make our political representatives more quickly and sensitively responsive to the people whose servants they are. More direct action by the people in their own affairs under proper safeguards is vitally neces-sary. The direct primary is a step in this direction, if it is associated with a corrupt-practices act effective to prevent the advantage of the man willing reck-lessly and unscrupulously to spend money over his more honest competitor. It is particularly important that all mon-eys received or expended for campaign purposes should be publicly accounted for, not only after election, but before election as well. Political action must be made simpler, easier, and freer from confusion for every citizen. I believe that the prompt removal of unfaithful or incompetent public servants should be made easy and sure in whatever way experience shall show to be most expedi-ent in any given class of cases.

One of the fundamental necessities in a representative government such as ours is to make certain that the men to whom the people delegate their power shall serve the people by whom they are elected, and not the special interests. I believe that every national officer, elected or appointed, should be forbidden to perform any service or receive any compensation, directly or indirectly, from interstate corporations; and a similar provision could not fail to be useful within the States.

The object of government is the welfare of the people. The material progress and prosperity of a nation are desirable chiefly so far as they lead to the moral and material welfare of all good citizens. Just in proportion as the average man and woman are honest, capable of sound judgment and high ideals, active in public affairs—but, first of all, sound in their home life, and the father and mother of healthy children whom they bring up well—just so far, and no farther, we may count our civilization a success. We must have—I believe we have already—a genuine and permanent moral awakening, without which no wisdom of legislation or administration really means anything; and, on the other hand, we must try to secure the social and economic legislation without which any improvement due to purely moral agitation is necessarily evanescent. [. . .]

So it is in our civil life. No matter how honest and decent we are in our private lives, if we do not have the right kind of law and the right kind of administration of the law, we cannot go forward as a nation. That is imperative; but it must be an addition to, and not a substitution for, the qualities that make us good citizens. In the last analysis, the most important elements in any man's career must be the sum of those qualities which, in the aggregate, we speak of as character. If he has not got it, then no law that the wit of man can devise, no administration of the law by the boldest and strongest executive, will avail to help him. We must have the right kind of character—character that makes a man, first of all, a good man in the home, a good father, a good husband—that makes a man a good neighbor. You must have that, and,

The New Nationalism was no mere campaign platform hastily written to win votes. It was rather the evolution of Theodore Roosevelt's political thought. His Osawatomie speech, in which he urged Americans to embrace a New Nationalism "to deal with new problems" ranks as one of his most important political discourses. New Nationalism, which Roosevelt defined as putting the "national need before sectional or personal advantage," identified most of his subsequent political career.

During the last years of his presidency, Roosevelt's political philosophy had evolved—he now conceptualized the federal government as a dynamic force in the social and economic life of its citizens. By 1909, he had adopted a program demanding broad federal economic and social regulations. It is impossible to determine the influence of Herbert Croly's seminal *Promise of American Life* (1909) on Roosevelt. He read the book with enthusiastic approval and he at once began to synthesize Croly's heavy language into political principles that the average citizen could understand. Basically, on one hand, Hamiltonian political thought believed that government should intervene directly to change existing economic relationships and/or to establish new ones. In the popular mind, Hamiltonianism became associated with the privileged. However, Jeffersonian political thought stressed that government should pursue a policy of strict *laissez faire* with regard to economic activity. In the popular mind, this implied a weak central government which chiefly functioned to promote democracy through a program of equal rights and opportunities. What Roosevelt—and Croly—now advocated was that progressives abandon their Jeffersonian prejudices against strong government and adopt Hamiltonian means to achieve Jeffersonian ends. In general, this was the theme that Roosevelt set forth during the campaign of 1912.

then, in addition, you must have the kind of law and the kind of administration of the law which will give to those qualities in the private citizen the best possible chance for development. The prime problem of our nation is to get the right type of good citizenship, and, to get it, we must have progress, and our public men must be genuinely progressive.

Taft Accepts the Nomination

The struggle between Taft and Roosevelt for the 1912 Republican nomination split the party. By the end of the primaries—30 states held them—there was no doubt that the rank and file wanted Roosevelt. But Taft controlled the party machinery that included the South and other boss-controlled delegations. When it was obvious that the conservatives were going to steal the nomination, most of Roosevelt's delegates withdrew from the June convention and agreed with their hero to return to Chicago at the beginning of August to organize the new Progressive Party.

Taft knew he had lost the election. He now considered it more important to purge the Republican Party of the increasingly radical progressives supporting Roosevelt. By obtaining the nomination, Taft guaranteed that his rival would never again control the party's leadership. Taft also attempted to preserve the Republican Party as a bastion of constitutional conservatism—and in doing so, affected Republican thought for the next generation.

Taft's letter accepting the 1912 nomination became the blueprint for Republican policies under future Presidents Harding, Coolidge, and Hoover—and his arguments were the conservative justification for the opposition to Franklin D. Roosevelt's New Deal (1933–45).

I accept the nomination which you tender me. I do so with profound gratitude to the Republican Party, which has thus honored me twice. I accept it as an approval of what I have done under its mandate, and as an expression of confidence that in a second Administration I will serve the public well. The issue presented to the convention, over which your Chairman presided with such a just and even hand, made a crises in the party's life. A faction sought to force the party to violate a valuable and time-honored National tradition by intrusting the power of the Presidency for more than two terms to one man, and that man one whose recently avowed political views would have committed the party to radical proposals involving dangerous changes in our present constitutional form of representative government and our independent judiciary.

This occasion is appropriate for the expression of profound gratitude at the victory or the right which was won at Chicago. By that victory the Republican Party was saved for future usefulness. It has been the party through which, substantially all the progress and development in our country's history in the last fifty years has been finally effected. It carried the country through the war which saved the Union, and through the greenback and silver crazes to a sound gold basis, which saved the country's honor and credit. It fought the Spanish war and successfully solved the new problem of our island possessions. It met the incidental evils of the enormous trade expansion and extended combinations of capital from 1897 until now by a successful crusade against the attempt of concentrated wealth to control the country's politics and its trade. It enacted regulatory legislation to make the railroads the servants and not the masters of the people. It has enforced the anti-trust laws until those who were not content with anything but monopolistic control of various branches of industry are now acquiescent in any plan which shall give them scope for legitimate expansion and assure them immunity from reckless prosecution.

The Republican Party has been alive to the modern change in the view of the duty of Government toward the people. Time was when, the least government was thought the best, and the policy which left all to the individual, unmolested and unaided by Government, was deemed the wisest. Now the duty of Government by positive law to further equality of opportunity in respect of the weaker classes in their dealings with the stronger and more powerful is clearly recognized. It is in this direction that real progress toward the greater human happiness is being made. [. . .]

The list of legislative enactments for the uplifting of those of our people suffering a disadvantage in their social and economic relation to others enacted by the Republican Party in this and previous Administrations is a long one, and shows the party sensitive to the needs of the people under the new view of Governmental responsibility.

Thus there was the pure food law and the meat inspection law to hold those who deal with the food of millions to a strict accountability for its healthful condition.

The frightful loss of life and limb to railway employees in times past has now been greatly reduced by statutes requiring safety appliances and proper inspection, of which two important ones were passed in this Administration.

The dreadful mining disasters in which thousands of miners met their death have led to a Federal Mining Bureau and generous appropriations to further discovery of methods for reducing explosions and other dangers in mining.

The statistics as to infant mortality and as to the too early employment of children in factories have prompted the creation of a children's bureau, by which the whole public can be made aware of actual conditions in the States and the best methods of reforming them for the saving and betterment of the coming generation.

The passage of time has brought the burdens and helplessness of old age to many of those veterans of the civil war who exposed their lives in the supreme struggle to save the Nation, and, recognizing this, Congress has added to

1908 poster. An artist's blend of Roosevelt and Taft likenesses. By 1912, clear lines were drawn, forever distinguishing the two candidates.

previous provision which patriotic gratitude had prompted a substantial allowance, which may be properly characterized as an old man's pension.

By the white slave act we have sought to save unfortunates from their own degradation and have forbidden the use of inter-State commerce in prompting vice.

In the making of the contract of employment between a railway employee and the company, the two do not stand on an equality, and the terms of the contract which the common law implied were unfair to the employee. Congress, in the exercise of its control over inter-State commerce, has reformed the contract to be implied and has made it more favorable to the employee. indeed, a more radical bill, which I fully approve, has passed the Senate and is now pending in the House which requires inter-State railways in effect to insure the lives of their employees and to make provision for prompt settlement of the amount due under the law after death or injury has occurred.

By the railroad legislation of this Administration, shippers have been placed much nearer an equality with the railroad whose lines they use than ever before. Rates cannot be increased except after the Inter-State Commerce Commission shall hold the increase reasonable. Orders against railways which under previous acts might be stayed by judicial injunction that involved delay of two years can now be examined and finally passed on by the

Commerce Court in about six months. Patrons of express, telegraph, and telephone companies may now secure reasonable rates by complaint to the commission. [. . .]

Congress has sought to encourage the movement toward eight hours a day for all manual labor by the recent enactment of a new law on the subject more stringent in its provisions regarding works on Government contracts.

One of the great defects in our present system of government is the delay and expense of litigation, which, of course, works against the poor litigant. The Supreme Court is now engaged in a revision of the equity rules to accomplish this purpose as to half our Federal litigation. The Workmen's Compensation act will relieve our courts of law of a very heavy part of the present dockets on the law side of the court and give the court more opportunity to speed the remaining causes. The last Congress codified the Federal court provisions, and we may look for, and should insist upon, a reform in the law procedure so as to promote dispatch of business and reduction in costs.

We have adopted in this Administration, after very considerable opposition, the postal savings banks, which work directly in the promotion of thrift among the people. By payment of only 2 per cent interest on deposits they do not compete with the savings banks. But they do attract those who fear banks and are unwilling to trust their funds except to a governmental agency. Experience, however, leads depositors to a knowledge of the importance of interest, and then seeking a higher rate, they transfer their accounts to the savings banks. In this way the savings bank deposits, instead of being reduced, are increased, and there is thus available a much larger fund for general investment. [. . .]

Celluloid Taft buttons

We are considering the changing needs of the people in the disposition of our public lands and their conservation. As those lands owned by the Government and useful for agricultural purposes which remain are, as a whole, less desirable as homesteads than those which have been already settled, it has been properly thought wise to reduce the time for perfecting a homestead claim from five years to three, and this whether on land within the rain area or in those arid tracts within the reclamation system.

Again a bill has passed the Senate, and is likely to pass the House, which will not compel the settlers on reclamation lands to wait ten years and until full payment of what they owe the Government before they receive title, but which gives a title after three years with a first Government lien.

On the other hand, the withdrawal of coal lands, phosphate lands, and oil lands and water-power sites is still maintained until Congress shall provide on the principles of proper conservation a system of disposition which will attract capital on the one hand and retain sufficient control by the Government on the other to prevent the evil of concentrating absolute ownership in a few persons of those sources for the production of necessities. [. . .]

We are living in an age in which, by exaggeration of the defects of our present condition, by false charges of responsibility for it against individuals and classes, by holding up to the feverish imagination of the less fortunate and the discontented the possibilities of a millennium, a condition of popular unrest has been produced. New parties are being formed, with the proposed purpose of satisfying this unrest by promising a panacea. In so far as inequality of condition can be lessened and equality of opportunity can be promoted by improvement of our educational system, the betterment of the laws to insure the quick administration of justice, and by the prevention of the acquisition of privilege without just compensation, in so far as the adoption of the legislation above recited and laws of a similar character may aid the less fortunate in their struggle with the hardships of life, all are in sympathy with a continued effort to remedy injustice and to aid the weak, and I venture to say that there is no National Administration in which more real steps of such progress have been taken than in the present one. But in so far as the propaganda for the satisfaction of unrest involves the promise of a millennium, a condition in which the rich are to be made reasonably poor and the poor reasonably rich by law, we are chasing a phantom: we are holding out to those whose unrest we fear a prospect and a dream, a vision of the impossible.

In the ultimate analysis, I fear, the equal opportunity which those seek who proclaim the coming of so-called social justice involves a forced division of property, and that means socialism. In the abuses of the last two decades it is true that ill-gotten wealth has been concentrated in some undeserving hands, and that if it were possible to redistribute it on any equitable principle to those from whom it was taken without adequate or proper compensation it would be a good result to bring about. But this is obviously impossible and impracticable. All that can be done is to treat this as one incidental evil of a great expansive movement in the material progress of the world and to make sure that there will be no recurrence of such evil. In this regard we have made great progress and reform, as in respect to secret rebates in railways, the improper conferring of public franchises, and the immunity of monopolizing trusts and combinations. The misfortunes of ordinary business, the division of the estates of wealthy men at their death, the chances of speculation which undue good fortune seems often to stimulate, operating as causes through a generation, will do much to divide up such large fortunes. It is far better to await the diminution of this evil by natural causes than to attempt what would soon take on the aspect of confiscation, or to abolish the principle and institution of private property and to change to socialism. Socialism involves the taking away of the motive for acquisition, saving, energy, and enterprise, and a futile attempt by committees to apportion the rewards due for productive labor. lt means stagnation and retrogression. It destroys the mainspring of human action that has carried the world on and upward for 2,000 years.

I do not say that the two gentlemen who now lead, one the Democratic

Party and the other the former Republicans who have left their party, in their attacks upon existing conditions, and in their attempt to satisfy the popular unrest by promises of remedies, are consciously embracing Socialism. The truth is that they do not offer any definite legislation or policy by which the happy conditions they promise are to be brought about, but if their promises mean anything, they lead directly toward the appropriation of what belongs to one man to another. The truth is, my friends, both those who have left the Republican Party under the inspiration of their present leader, and our old opponents, the Democrats, under their candidate, are going in a direction they do not definitely know, toward an end they cannot definitely describe, with but one chief and clear object, and that is of acquiring power for their party by popular

Sized cotton banner with a portrait of Taft encircled by an oak wreath.

support through the promise of a change for the better. What they clamor for is a change. They ask for a change in government so that the Government may be restored to the people, as if this had not been a people's Government since the beginning of the Constitution. I have the fullest sympathy with every reform in governmental and election machinery which shall facilitate the expression of the popular will, as the short ballot and the reduction in elective offices to make it possible. But these gentlemen propose to reform the Government, whose present defects, if any, are due to the failure of the people to devote as much time as is necessary to their political duties by requiring a political activity by the people three times that which thus far the people have been willing to assume, and thus they propose remedies which, instead of exciting the people to further interest and activity in the Government, will tire them into such an indifference as still further to remand control of public affairs to a minority.

But after we have changed all the governmental machinery so as to permit instantaneous expression of the people in constitutional amendments, in statutes, and in recall of public agents, what then? Votes are not bread, constitutional amendments are not work, referendums do not pay rent or furnish houses, recalls do not furnish clothing, initiatives do not supply employment or relieve inequalities of condition or of opportunity. We still ought to have set before us the definite plans to bring on complete equality of opportunity, and to abolish hardship and evil for humanity. We listen for them in vain.

Instead of giving us the benefit of any specific remedies for the hardships and evils of society they point out, they follow their urgent appeals for closer association of the people in legislation by an attempt to cultivate the hostility of the people to the courts and to represent that they are in some form upholding injustice and are obstructing the popular will. Attempts are made to take away all those safeguards for maintaining the independence of the judiciary which are so carefully framed in our Constitution. These attempts find expression in the policy, on the one hand, of the recall of Judges, a system under which a Judge whose decision in one case may temporarily displease the electorate is to be deprived at once of his office by a popular vote, a pernicious system embodied in the Arizona Constitution and which the Democrats of the House and Senate refused to condemn as the initial policy of a new State. The same spirit manifested itself in the vote by Democratic Senators on the proposition, first, to abolish the Commerce Court, and, second, to abolish Judges by mere act of repeal, although under the Constitution their terms are for life, on no ground except that they did not like some of the court's recent decisions.

Another form of hostility to the judiciary is shown in the grotesque proposition by the leader of former Republicans who have left their party for a recall of decisions so that a decision on a point of constitutional law, having been rendered by the highest court capable of rendering it, shall then be submitted to popular vote to determine whether it ought to be sustained. Again, the Democratic Party in Congress and convention shows its desire to weaken the courts by forbidding the use of the writ of injunction to protect a lawful business against the destructive effect of a secondary boycott and by interposing a jury in contempt proceedings brought to enforce its order and decrees. These provisions are really class legislation designed to secure immunity for lawlessness in labor disputes on the part of the laborers, but operating much more widely to paralyze the arm of the court in cases which do not involve labor disputes at all. [. . .]

The Republican Party stands for none of these innovations. It refuses to make changes simply for the purpose of making a change, and cultivating popular hope that in the change something beneficial, undefined, will take place. It does not believe that human nature has changed. It still believes that it is possible in this world that the fruits of energy, courage, enterprise, attention to duty, hard work, thrift, providence, restraint of appetite and of passions will continue to have their reward under our present system, and that laziness, lack of attention, lack of industry, the yielding to appetite and passion, carelessness, dishonesty, and disloyalty will ultimately find their own punishment in the world here. We do not deny that there are exceptions and that seeming fortune follows wickedness and misfortune virtue, but, on the whole, we are optimists and believe that the rule is the other way. We do not know any way to avoid human injustice but to perfect our laws for administering justice, to develop the morality of the individual, to give direct supervision and aid to those who are, or are likely to be, oppressed, and to give as full scope as possible to individual effort and its rewards.

Wherever we can see a statute which does not deprive any person or class of what is his is going to help many people, we are in favor of it. We favor the greatest good to the greatest number, but we do not believe that this can be accomplished by minimizing the rewards of individual effort, or by infringing or destroying the right of property, which. next to the right of liberty, has been and is the greatest civilizing institution in history. In other words, the Republican Party believes in progress along the lines upon which we have

WM. H. TAFT

Theodore Roosevelt

Silk ribbons for Taft and Roosevelt. After the epic struggle of 1912, the two men remained extremely cool to each other. Each attacked the other in books and articles. On an expedition to Brazil (1914), Roosevelt explored areas which had been blank spaces on the map. At the outbreak of World War I (1914), he favored the Allies and criticized Wilson's neutrality program. Roosevelt died in 1919. Taft served as professor of law at Yale (1913–21). He was appointed Chief Justice of the United States Supreme Court by President Warren Harding in 1921, a position he held until his death in 1930.

attained progress already. We do not believe that we can reach a millennium by a sudden change in all our existing institutions. We believe that we have made progress from the beginning until now, and that the progress is to continue into the far future: that it is reasonable progress that experience has shown to be really useful and helpful, and from which there is no reaction to something worse.

The Republican Party stands for the Constitution as it is, with such amendments adopted according to its provisions as new conditions thoroughly understood may require. We believe that it has stood the test of time and that there have been disclosed really to serious defects in its operation.

It is said that this is not an issue in the campaign. It seems to me it is the supreme issue. The Democratic Party and the former Republicans who have left their party are neither of them to be trusted on this subject, as I have shown. The Republican Party is the nucleus of that public opinion which favors constant progress and development along safe and sane lines and under the Constitution as we have had it for more than 100 years, and which believes in the maintenance of an independent judiciary as the keystone of our liberties and the balance wheel by which the whole governmental machinery is kept within the original plan.

The normal and logical question which ought to be asked and answered in determining whether an Administration should be continued in power is, How has the Government been administered? Has it been economical and efficient? Has it sided or obstructed business prosperity? Has it made for progress in bettering the condition of the people, and especially of the wage earner? Ought its general policies to approve themselves to the people?

During this Administration we have given special attention to the machinery of government with a view to increasing its efficiency and reducing its cost. For 10 years there has been a continuous expansion in every direction of the governmental functions and a necessary increase in the civil and military servants of whom these functions are performed. The expenditures of the Government have normally increased from year to year on an average of nearly 1 per cent. There never has been a systematic investigation and reorganization of this governmental structure with a view to eliminating duplications, to uniting bureaus where union is possible and more effective, and to making the whole organization more compact and its parts more closely coordinated. As a beginning, we examined closely the estimates. These, unless watched, grow from year to year under the natural tendency of the bureau chiefs. The first estimates which were presented to use we cut some $50,000,000, and this policy we have maintained through the Administration, and have prevented the normal annual increase in Government expenditures, so the result is that the deficit of $58,785,000, which we found on the 1st of July, 1909, was changed on the 1st of July, 1910, by increase of the revenues under the Payne law, including the corporation tax, to a surplus of $15,806,000, on July 1, 1911, to a surplus of $47,284,000, and on July 1,1912, to a surplus of $86,886,000. The expenditures for 1909 were $662,824,000; for 1910, $630,703,000; for 1911, $654,188,000, and for 1912 were $634,804,000. These figures of surplus and expenditure do not include any receipts or expenditures on account of the Panama Canal.

I secured an appropriation for the appointment of an Economy and Efficiency Commission consisting of the ablest experts in the country, and they have been working for two years on the question of how the Government may be reorganized and what changes can be made with a view to giving it greater effectiveness for governmental purposes on the one hand and securing this at considerably less cost on the other. I have transmitted to Congress from time to time the recommendations of this commission, and while they cannot all be adopted at one session, and while their recommendations have not been rounded and complete because of the necessity for taking greater time, I think that the Democratic Appropriation Committee of the House has become convinced that we are on the right road and that substantial reform may be effected through the adoption of most of the plans recommended by this commission.

For the benefit of our own people and of the world we have carried on the work of the Panama Canal, so that we can now look forward with confidence to its completion within eighteen months. The work has been a remarkable one, and has involved the expenditure of $30,000,000 to $40,000,000 annually for a series of years, and yet it has been attended with no scandal, and with a development of such engineering and medical skill and ingenuity as to command the admiration of the world and to bring the highest credit to our Corps of Army Engineers and our Army Medical Corps.

In our foreign relations we have maintained peace everywhere and sought to promote its continuance and permanence. [. . .]

During this Administration everything that has been possible has been done to increase our foreign trade, and under the Payne bill the maximum and minimum clause furnished the opportunity for removing discriminations in that trade, so that the statistics show that our exports and imports reached, for the year ending July 1, 1912, a higher figure than ever before in the history of the country. Our imports for the last fiscal year ending July 1, 1912, amounted to $1,658,426,174 and our exports to $2,049,820,199, or a total of $8,857,648,262. If there were added to this the business done with Porto Rico, Hawaii, and the Philippines the sum total of our foreign trade would considerably exceed $4,000,000,000. The excess of our exports over imports is $550,795,914. Manufactures exported during the year 1912 exceeded $1,000,000,000, and surpass the previous record. These figures seem to show that the business is large enough to produce prosperity, and the fact is that it has done so.

The platform of 1908 promised, on behalf of the Republican Party, to do certain things. One was that the tariff would be revised at an extra session. An extra session was called and the tariff was revised. [. . .]

If the result of the election were to put the Democrats completely in control of all branches of the Government, then we may look for the reduction of duties upon all those articles the manufacture of which need protection, and may anticipate a serious injury to a large part of our manufacturing industry. We would not have to wait for actual legislation on this subject: the very prospect of Democratic success, when its policy toward our great protected industries became understood, would postpone indefinitely the coming of prosperity and tend to give us a recurrence of the hard times that we had in the decade between 1890 and 1897. The Democratic platform declares protection to be unconstitutional, although it has been the motive and purpose of most tariff bills since 1789, and indicates as clearly as possible the intention to depart from a protective policy at once. It is true the Democratic platform says that the change to the policy of a revenue tariff is to be made in such a way as not to injure industry. This is utterly impossible when we are on a protective basis, and it is conclusively shown to be so by the necessary effect of bills already introduced and passed by the Democratic House for the purpose of making strides toward a revenue tariff. It is now more than fifteen years since the people of this country have had an experience in such a change as that which the coming in of the Democratic Party would involve. It ought to be brought home to the people as clearly as possible that a change of economic policy, such as that which is deliberately proposed in the Democratic platform, would halt many of our manufacturing enterprises and throw many wage earners out of employment, would injure much the home markets which the farmers now enjoy for their products, and produce a condition of suffering among the people that no reforming legislation could neutralize or mitigate.

The statement has been widely circulated and has received considerable support from political opponents, that the Tariff act of 1909 is a prominent factor in creating the high cost of living. This is not true. A careful investigation will show that the phenomenon of increased prices and cost of living is world-wide in its extent, and quite as much in evidence in other countries of advanced civilization and progressive tendencies as in our own. Bitter complaints of the burden of increased prices and cost of living have been made not only in this country, but even in countries of Asia and Africa. Disorder and even riots have occurred in several European cities because of the unprecedented cost of food products. [. . .]

It is difficult to understand how any legislation or promise in a political platform can remedy this universal condition. I have recommended the creation of a commission to study this subject and to report upon all possible methods for alleviating the hardship of which the people complain, but great economic tendencies, notable among which are the practically universal movement from the country to the city and the increased supply of gold, have been the most potent factors in causing high prices. These facts every careful student of the situation must admit.

There is one respect in which high tariff rates may make for exorbitant prices. If the rate is higher than the difference between the cost of production here and abroad, then it tempts the manufacturers of this country to secure monopoly of the industry and to increase its price as far as the excessive tariff will permit. The danger may be avoided in two ways: First, by carefully adjusting the tariff on articles needing protection so that the manufacturer secures only enough protection to pay the scale of high wages which obtains and ought to obtain in this country and secure a reasonable profit from the business. This may be done by the continuance of the Tariff Board's investigation into the facts, which will enable Congress and the people to know what the tariff as to each schedule ought to be. The American public may rest assured that should the Republican Party be restored to power in all legislative branches, all the schedules in the present tariff of which complaint is made will be subjected to investigation and report by a competent and impartial Tariff Board and to the reduction or change which may be necessary to square the rates with the facts.

The other method of avoiding danger of excessive prices from excessive duties is to enforce the anti-trust law against those who combine to take advantage of the excessive tariff rates. This brings me to the discussion of the Sherman act.

The anti-trust law was passed to provide against the organization and maintenance of combinations for the manufacture and sale of commodities, which, through restraint of trade, either by contract and agreement or by various methods of unfair competition, should suppress competition, establish monopoly, and control prices. The measure has been on the statute book since 1890, and many times under construction by the courts, but not until the litigation against the Standard Oil Company and against the American Tobacco Company reached the Supreme Court did the statute receive an authoritative construction which is workable and intelligible.

It would aid the business public if specific acts of unfair trade which characterize the establishment of unlawful monopolies should be denounced as misdemeanors for the purpose, first, of making plainer to the public what must be avoided, and, second, for the purpose of punishing such acts by summary procedure without the necessity for the formidable array of witnesses and the lengthy trials essential to establish a general conspiracy under the present act. But there is great need for other constructive legislation of a helpful kind. Combination of capital in great enterprises should be encouraged, if within the law, for every one must recognize that progress in modern business is by effective combination of the means of production to the point of greatest economy. It should be our purpose, therefore, to put large inter-State business enterprises acting within the law on a basis of security by offering them a Federal corporation law under which they may voluntarily incorporate. Such an act is not an easy one to draw in detail, but its general outlines are clearly defined by the two objects of such a law. One is to secure for the public through competent Government agency, such a close supervision and regulation of the business transactions of the corporation as to preclude a violation of the anti-trust and other laws to which the business of the corporation must square, and the other is to furnish to business, thus incorporated and lawfully conducted, the protection and security which it must enjoy under such a Federal charter. With the faculties conferred by such a charter corporations could do business in all the States without complying with conflicting exceptions of State Legislatures, and could be sure of uniform taxation i.e. uniforms with that imposed by the State on State corporations in the same business.

I am not in sympathy with the purpose to make the anti-trust law more drastic by such a provision as is proposed by the Democratic majority of the investigating Committee of the House for imposing a rule as to burden of proof upon defendants under anti-trust prosecution different from that which defendants in other prosecutions enjoy. This cannot be suggested by any difficulty found in proving to the courts the illegality of such combinations when the illegality exists. I challenge the production of a single record in any case in which an objectionable combination has escaped a decree against it because of any favorable role as to the burden of proof. It is true that many defendants in criminal cases have escaped by a failure of the jury to convict, but that arises from the reluctance and refusal of jurors to find verdicts upon which men are likely to be sent to the penitentiary for pursuing a course in business competition which the ordinary man did not regard as immoral or criminal before the passage of the act.

I think I may affirm without contradiction that the prosecution of all persons reported to the Department of Justice to have violated the anti-trust law has been carried on in this Administration without fear or favor, and that every one who has violated it, no matter how prominent or how great his influence, has been brought before the bar of the court either in criminal or civil suit to answer the charge. [. . .]

I have thus outlined [. . .] what I consider to be the able issues of this campaign. There are others of importance, but time does not permit me to discuss them. [. . .] For the present it is sufficient for me to say that it is greatly in the interest of the people to maintain the solidarity of the Republican Party for future usefulness and to continue it and its policies in control of the destinies of the Nation. I cannot think that the American people after the scrutiny and education of a three months' campaign, during which they will be able to see through the fog of misrepresentation and demagoguery, will fail to recognize that the two great issues which are here presented to them are first, whether we shall retain, on a sound and permanent basis, our popular constitutional representative form of government, with the independence of the judiciary as a necessary key to the preservation of those liberties that are the inheritance of 1,000 years, and, second, whether we shall welcome prosperity which is just at our door by maintaining our present economic business basis and by the encouragement of business expansion and progress through legitimate use of capital. [. . .]

Progressive Party Platform of 1912

The Progressive or Bull Moose Party, as it was more familiarly known, was conceived on June 20, 1912, at a meeting in Chicago of Theodore Roosevelt's chief advisors. Officially, it was created the following night when Roosevelt told a tumultuous gathering that he would accept the presidential nomination of the party.

The Progressive platform called for the establishment of a democratized and powerful social service state which foreshadowed Franklin Roosevelt's New Deal. The entire document contained a myriad of proposals to make government more responsive to the will of the people. To pay for these extended services, the Progressive platform implicitly promised some redistribution of wealth by advocating steeply graduated inheritance and income taxes.

Declaration of Principles of the Progressive Party

The conscience of the people, in a time of grave national problems, has called into being a new party, born of the Nation's awakened sense of justice. We of the Progressive Party here dedicate ourselves to the fulfillment of the duty laid upon us by our fathers to maintain that government of the people, by the people and for the people whose foundation they laid.

We hold with Thomas Jefferson and Abraham Lincoln that the people are the masters of their Constitution, to fulfill its purposes and to safeguard it from those who, by perversion of its intent, would convert it into an instrument of injustice. In accordance with the needs of each generation the people must use their sovereign powers to establish and maintain equal opportunity and industrial justice, to secure which this Government was founded and without which no republic can endure.

This country belongs to the people who inhabit it. Its resources, its business, its institutions and its laws should be utilized, maintained or altered in whatever manner will best promote the general interest.

It is time to set the public welfare in the first place.

The Old Parties

Political parties exist to secure responsible government and to execute the will of the people.

From these great tasks both of the old parties have turned aside. Instead of instruments to promote the general welfare, they have become the tools of corrupt interests which use them impartially to serve their selfish purposes. Behind the ostensible government sits enthroned an invisible government, owing no allegiance and acknowledging no responsibility to the people.

To destroy this invisible government, to dissolve the unholy alliance

Selection of Roosevelt celluloid buttons with "Hat in the Ring" imagery. Many pins, postcards, and buttons celebrated this statement made when he declared his third-party candidacy.

between corrupt business and corrupt politics is the first task of the statesmanship of the day.

The deliberate betrayal of its trust by the Republican Party, and the fatal incapacity of the Democratic Party to deal with the new issues of the new time, have compelled the people to forge a new instrument of government through which to give effect to their will in laws and institutions.

Unhampered by tradition, uncorrupted by power, undismayed by the magnitude of the task, the new party offers itself as the instrument of the people to sweep away old abuses, to build a new and nobler commonwealth.

A Covenant with the People

This declaration is our covenant with the people, and we hereby bind the party and its candidates in State and Nation to the pledges made herein.

The Rule of the People

The Progressive Party, committed to the principle of government by a self-controlled democracy expressing its will through representatives of the people, pledges itself to secure such alterations in the fundamental law of the several States and of the United States as shall insure the representative character of the Government.

In particular, the party declares for direct primaries for nomination of State and National officers, for Nation-wide preferential primaries for candidates for the Presidency, for the direct election of United States Senators by the people; and we urge on the States the policy of the short ballot, with responsibility to the people secured by the initiative, referendum and recall. [. . .]

Social and Industrial Strength

The supreme duty of the Nation is the conservation of human resources through an enlightened measure of social and industrial justice. We pledge ourselves to work unceasingly in State and Nation for:

- Effective legislation looking to the prevention of industrial accidents, occupational diseases, overwork, involuntary unemployment, and other injurious effects incident to modern industry;
- The fixing of minimum safety and health standards for the various occupations, and the exercise of the public authority of State and Nation, including the Federal control over inter-State commerce and the taxing power, to maintain such standards;
- The prohibition of child labor;
- Minimum wage standards for working women, to provide a living scale in all industrial occupations;
- The prohibition of night work for women and the establishment of an eight hour day for women and young persons;
- One day's rest in seven for all wage-workers;

• The abolition of the convict contract labor system, substituting a system of prison production for governmental consumption only, and the application of prisoners' earnings to the support of their dependent families;

• Publicity as to wages, hours and conditions, and labor; full reports upon industrial accidents and diseases, and the opening to public inspection of all tallies, weights, measures, and check systems on labor products;

• Standards of compensation for death by industrial accident and injury and trade diseases which will transfer the burden of lost earnings from the families of working people to the industry, and thus to the community;

• The protection of home life against the hazards of sickness, irregular employment and old age through the adoption of a system of social insurance adapted to American use;

• The development of the creative labor power of America by lifting the last load of illiteracy from American youth and establishing continuation schools for industrial education under public control and encouraging agricultural education and demonstration in rural schools;

• The establishment of industrial research laboratories to put the methods and discoveries of science at the service of American producers.

We favor the organization of the workers, men and women, as a means of protecting their interests and of promoting their progress.

Business

We believe that true popular government, justice, and prosperity go hand in hand, and so believing, it is our purpose to secure that large measure of general prosperity which is the fruit of legitimate and honest business, fostered by equal justice and by sound progressive laws.

We demand that the test of true prosperity shall be the benefits conferred thereby on all the citizens not confined to individuals or classes and that the test of corporate efficiency shall be the ability better to serve the public; that those who profit by control of business affairs shall justify that profit and that control by sharing with the public the fruits thereof.

We therefore demand a strong National regulation of inter-State corporations. The corporation is an essential part of modern business. The concentration of modern business, in some degree, is both inevitable and necessary for National and international business efficiency. but the existing concentration of vast wealth under a corporate system, unguarded and uncontrolled by the Nation, has placed in the hands of a few men enormous, secret,

Lithographed tin game. The directions read: "The Teddy sideways glance makes the political bosses dance. To do this little stunt, make his eyes look straight in front. Then you vote and I'll vote and with other votes galore we'll land the Bull Moose President within the White House door."

irresponsible power over the daily life of the citizen—a power insufferable in a free government and certain of abuse.

This power has been abused, in monopoly of National resources, in stock watering, in unfair competition and unfair privileges, and finally in sinister influences on the public agencies of State and Nation. We do not fear commercial power, but we insist that it shall be exercised openly, under publicity, supervision and regulation of the most efficient sort, which will preserve its good while eradicating and preventing its evils.

To that end we urge the establishment of a strong Federal administrative commission of high standing, which shall maintain permanent active super-

ROOSEVELT

PROGRESSIVE CONVENTION

LINCOLN, NEBR.
September 3, 1912

Silk ribbon with Roosevelt photograph. On August 5, 1912, the Progressive Party met in a national convention in Chicago and nominated Roosevelt. Throughout the next month, state conventions ratified the choice.

vision over industrial corporations engaged in inter-State commerce, or such of them as are of public importance, doing for them what the Government now does for the National banks, and what is now done for the railroads by the Inter-State Commerce Commission.

Such a commission must enforce the complete publicity of those corporation transactions which are of public interest; must attack unfair competition, false capitalization, and special privilege, and by continuous trained watchfulness guard and keep open equally to all the highways of American commerce.

Thus the business man will have certain knowledge of the law, and will be able to conduct his business easily in conformity therewith; the investor will find security for his capital; dividends will be rendered more certain, and the savings of the people will be drawn naturally and safely into the channels of trade.

Under such a system of constructive regulation, legitimate business, freed from confusion, uncertainty and fruitless litigation, will develop normally in response to the energy and enterprise of the American business man.

We favor strengthening the Sherman law by prohibiting agreements to divide territory or limit output; refusing to sell to customers who buy from business rivals; to sell below cost in certain areas while maintaining higher prices in other places; using the power of transportation to aid or injure special business concerns; and other unfair trade practices.

Commercial Development

The time has come when the Federal Government should co-operate with the manufacturers and producers in extending our foreign commerce. To this end we demand adequate appropriations by Congress and the appointment of diplomatic and consular officers solely with a view to their special fitness and worth, and not in consideration of political expediency.

It is imperative to the welfare of our people that we enlarge and extend our foreign commerce. We are pre-eminently fitted to do this because as a people we have developed high skill in the art of manufacturing; our business men are strong executives, strong organizers. In every way possible our Federal Government should co-operate in this important matter. Anyone who has had the opportunity to study and observe first-hand Germany's course in this respect must realize that their policy of co-operation between Government and business has in comparatively few years made them a leading competitor for the commerce of the world. It should be remembered that they are doing this on a national scale and with large units of business, while the Democrats would have us believe that we should do it with small units of business, which would be controlled not by the National Government but by forty-nine conflicting sovereignties. Such a policy is utterly out of keeping with the progress of the times and gives our great commercial rivals in Europe—hungry for international markets—golden opportunities of which they are rapidly taking advantage. [. . .]

Debs's Speech to the Socialist Party

Under the leadership of Eugene V. Debs (1855–1926), the Socialist Party made remarkable strides. In 1900, it had about 10,000 members. In 1904, with Debs as the presidential candidate, the party polled more than 400,000 votes—three percent of the total. In 1912, the Socialists scored their highest presidential vote. Debs received about 900,000 ballots or six percent of the total—even during the collapse of the capitalist system in 1932, the socialist movement never matched that early success. In 1912, many believed that American socialism was on the eve of the kind of success that had made European social democracy a mass movement. However, the unique American political, economic, and social experience obviously worked against socialism.

Eugene V. Debs delivered this explanation of American socialism, its philosophy and goals, when he accepted the party's 1912 presidential nomination.

The Socialist Party is fundamentally different from all other parties. It came in the process of evolution and grows with the growth of the forces which created it. Its spirit is militant and its aim revolutionary. It expresses in political terms the aspiration of the working class to freedom and to a larger and fuller life than they have yet known.

The world's workers have always been and still are the world's slaves. They have borne all the burdens of the race and built all the monuments along the track of civilization; they have produced all the world's wealth and supported all the world's governments. They have conquered all things but their own freedom. They are still the subject class in every nation on earth and the chief function of every government is to keep them at the mercy of their masters.

The workers in the mills and factories, in the mines and on the farms and railways never had a party of their own until the Socialist Party was organized. They divided their votes between the parties of their masters. They did not realize that they were using their ballots to forge their own fetters.

But the awakening came. It was bound to come. Class rule became more and more oppressive and wage slavery more and more galling. The eyes of the workers began to open. They began to see the cause of the misery they had dumbly suffered so many years. It dawned upon them that society was divided into two classes—capitalists and workers, exploiters and producers; that the capitalists, while comparatively few owned the nation and controlled the government; that the courts and the soldiers were at their command and that the workers, while in a great majority, were in slavish subjection.

When they ventured to protest they were discharged and found themselves blacklisted; when they went out on strike they were suppressed by the soldiers and sent to jail.

They looked about them and saw a land of wonderful resources: they saw the productive machinery made by their own hands and the vast wealth produced by their own labor, in the shadow of which their wives and children were perishing in the skeleton clutch of famine.

The very suffering they were forced to endure quickened their senses. They began to think. A new light dawned upon their dark skies. They rubbed the age-long sleep from their eyes. They had long felt the brutalizing effect of class rule; now they saw the cause of it. Slowly but steadily they became class-conscious. They said, "We are brothers, we are comrades," and they saw themselves multiplied by millions. They caught the prophetic battle-cry of Karl Marx, the world's greatest labor leader, the inspired evangel of working-class emancipation. "Workers of all countries, unite!"

And now, behold! The international Socialist movement spreads out over all the nations of the earth. The world's workers are aroused at last. They are no longer on their knees; their bowed bodies are now erect. Despair has given way to hope, weakness to strength, fear to courage. They no longer cringe and supplicate; they hold up their heads and command. They have ceased to fear their masters and have learned to trust themselves.

And this is how the Socialist Party came to be born. It was quickened into life in the bitter struggle of the world's enslaved workers. It expresses collective determination to break their fetters and emancipate themselves and the race.

Is it strange that the workers are loyal to such a party, that they proudly stand beneath its blazing banners and fearlessly proclaim its conquering principles? It is the one party of their class, born of their agony and baptized in the blood of their countless brethren who perished in the struggle to give it birth.

Hail to this great party of the toiling millions whose battle-cry is heard around the world!

We do not plead for votes; the workers give them freely the hour they understand.

But we need to destroy the prejudice that still exists and dispel the darkness that still prevails in the working class world. We need the clear light of sound education and the conquering power of economic and political organization.

Before the unified hosts of labor all the despotic governments on earth are powerless and all resistance vain. Before their onward march all ruling classes disappear and all slavery vanishes forever.

The appeal of the Socialist Party is to all the useful people of the nation, all who work with brain and muscle to produce the nation's wealth and who promote its progress and conserve its civilization.

Only they who bear its burdens may rightfully enjoy the blessings of civilized society.

There are no boundary lines to separate race from race, sex from sex or creed from creed in the Socialist Party. The common rights of all are equally recognized.

Every human being is entitled to sunlight and air, to what his labor produces, and to an equal chance with every other human being to unfold and ripen and give to the world the riches of his mind and soul.

Economic slavery is the world's greatest curse today. Poverty and misery, prostitution, insanity and crime are its inevitable results.

The Socialist Party is the one party which stands squarely and uncompromisingly for the abolition of industrial slavery; the one party pledged in every fibre of its being to the economic freedom of all the people.

So long as the nation's resources and productive and distributive machinery are the private property of a privileged class the masses will be at their mercy, poverty will be their lot and life will be shorn of all that raises it above the brute level.

The infallible test of a political party is the private ownership of the sources of wealth and the means of life. Apply that test to the Republican, Democratic, and Progressive parties and upon that basic, fundamental issue you will find them essentially one and the same. They differ according to the conflicting interests of the privileged classes, but at bottom they are alike and stand for capitalist class rule and working class slavery.

The new Progressive Party is a party of progressive capitalism. It is lavishly financed and shrewdly advertised. But it stands for the rule of capitalism all the same.

When the owners of the trusts finance a party to put themselves out of business: when they turn over their wealth to the people from whom they stole it and go to work for a living, it will be time enough to consider the merits of the Roosevelt Progressive Party.

One question is sufficient to determine the true status of all these parties. Do they want the workers to own the tools they work with, control their own jobs and secure to themselves the wealth they produce? Certainly not. That is utterly ridiculous and impossible from their point of view.

The Republican, Democratic, and Progressive parties all stand for the private ownership by the capitalists of the productive machinery used by the workers, so that the capitalists can continue to filch the wealth produced by the workers.

The Socialist Party is the only party which declares that the tools of labor belong to labor and that the wealth produced by the working class belong to the working class.

Intelligent workingmen are no longer deceived. They know that the struggle in which the world is engaged today is a class struggle and that in this struggle the workers can never win by giving their votes to capitalist parties. They have tried this for many years and it has always produced the same result to them.

The class of privilege and pelf has had the world by the throat and the working class beneath its iron-shod hoofs long enough. The magic word of freedom is ringing through the nation and the spirit of intelligent revolt is finding expression in every land beneath the sun.

The solidarity of the working class is the salient force in the social transformation of which we behold the signs upon every hand. Nearer and nearer they are being drawn together in the bonds of unionism: clearer and clearer becomes their collective vision; greater and greater the power that throbs within them.

They are the twentieth-century hosts of freedom who are to destroy all despotisms, topple over all thrones, seize all sceptres of authority and hold them in their own strong hands, tear up all privilege by the roots, and consecrate the earth and all its fullness to the joy and service of all humanity.

It is vain to hope for material relief upon the prevailing system of capitalism. All the reforms that are proposed by the three capitalist parties, even if carried out in good faith, would still leave the working class in industrial slavery.

The working class will never be emancipated by the grace of the capitalist class, but only by overthrowing that class.

The power to emancipate itself is inherent in the working class, and this power must be developed through sound education and applied through sound organization.

It is as foolish and self-destructive for workingmen to turn to Republican, Democratic and Progressive parties on election day as it would be for them to turn to the Manufacturers' Association and the Citizens' Alliance when they are striking against starvation wages.

The capitalist class is organized economically and politically to keep the working class in subjection and perpetuate its power as a ruling class. They do not support a working class union nor a working class party. They are not so foolish. They wisely look out for themselves.

The capitalist class despise a working class party. Why should the working class give their support to a capitalist class party?

Capitalist misrule under which workingmen suffer slavery and the most galling injustice exists only because it has workingmen's support. Withdraw that support and capitalism is dead.

The capitalists can enslave and rob the workers only by the consent of the workers when they cast their ballots on election day.

Every vote cast for a capitalist party, whatever its name, is a vote for wage-slavery, for poverty and degradation.

Every vote cast for the Socialist Party, the workers' own party, is a vote for emancipation.

We appeal to the workers and to all who sympathize with them to make their power felt in this campaign. Never before has there been so great an opportunity to strike an effective blow for freedom.

Capitalism is rushing blindly to its impending doom. All the signs portend the inevitable breakdown of the existing order. Deep-seated discontent has seized upon the masses. They must indeed be deaf who do not hear the mutterings of the approaching storm.

Poverty, high prices, unemployment, child slavery, widespread misery and haggard want in a land bursting with abundance: prostitution and insanity, suicide and crime, these in solemn numbers tell the tragic story of capitalism's saturnalia of blood and tears and shame as its end draws near.

It is to abolish this monstrous system and the misery and crime which flow from it in a direful and threatening stream that the Socialist Party was organized and now makes its appeal to the intelligence and conscience of the people. Social reorganization is the imperative demand of this world-wide revolutionary movement.

The Socialist Party's mission is not only to destroy capitalist despotism but to establish industrial and social democracy. To this end the workers are steadily organizing and fitting themselves for the day when they shall take control of the people's industries and when the right to work shall be as inviolate as the right to breathe the breath of life.

Standing as it does for the emancipation of the working class from wage-slavery, for the equal rights and opportunities of all men and all women, for

> Why did socialism in the United States fail to do what it has done in every other advanced industrial nation, i.e. win the working class to its banner and thus lay the foundations of a mass political party? The historians Charles and Mary Beard explained the failure of Eugene V. Debs and socialism in America this way:
>
> > Among the American working classes, all save the most wretched had aspirations; there was a baton in every toolkit. The public schools which flung wide for all the portals to the mysterious world of science, letters and art opened the way for the talented to rise into the professions—at least that of politics. No tokens of garb, tongue, accent or grammar marked them off as hopelessly from the upper reaches of society as the English cockney was separated from superior persons of Rotten Row. . . . There was misery enough, no doubt; there were occasional outbreaks of political unrest which seemed to indicate a class upheaval as occurred during Henry George's campaign [for mayor of New York] in 1886; there were strikes longer and bloodier than ever before; there were a few hole-in-the-corner anarchists who compared the assassination of Garfield with the murder of the Tsar, Alexander II; but there was no multitudinous, grim, sodden, submerged industrial mass beaten to the status of permanent servitude.
> >
> > —Charles and Mary Beard, *The Rise of American Civilization* (New York: Macmillan, 1947): p. 395

the abolition of child labor and the conservation of all childhood, for social self-rule and the equal freedom of all, the Socialist Party is the party of progress, the party of the future, and its triumph will signalize the birth of a new civilization and the dawn of a happier day for all humanity.

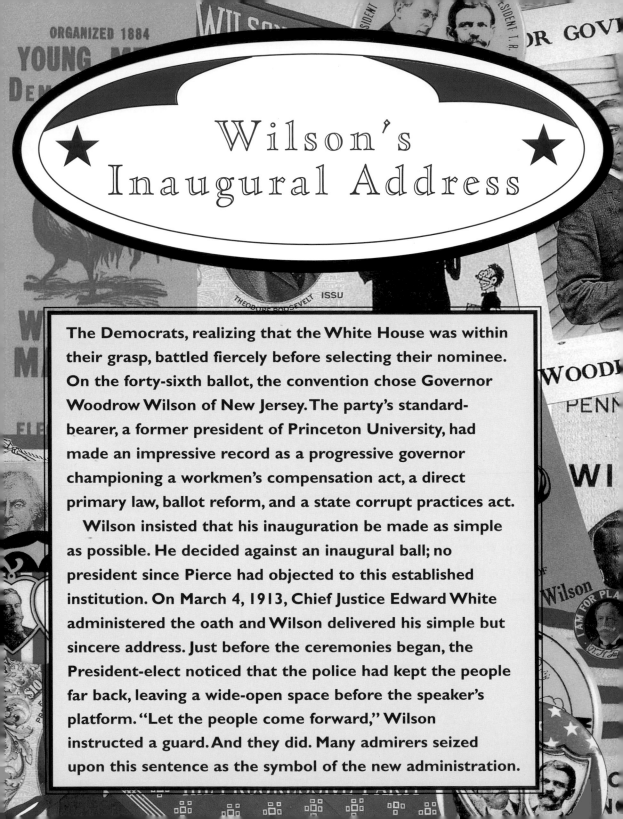

Wilson's Inaugural Address

The Democrats, realizing that the White House was within their grasp, battled fiercely before selecting their nominee. On the forty-sixth ballot, the convention chose Governor Woodrow Wilson of New Jersey. The party's standard-bearer, a former president of Princeton University, had made an impressive record as a progressive governor championing a workmen's compensation act, a direct primary law, ballot reform, and a state corrupt practices act.

Wilson insisted that his inauguration be made as simple as possible. He decided against an inaugural ball; no president since Pierce had objected to this established institution. On March 4, 1913, Chief Justice Edward White administered the oath and Wilson delivered his simple but sincere address. Just before the ceremonies began, the President-elect noticed that the police had kept the people far back, leaving a wide-open space before the speaker's platform. "Let the people come forward," Wilson instructed a guard. And they did. Many admirers seized upon this sentence as the symbol of the new administration.

There has been a change of government. It began two years ago, when the House of Representatives became Democratic by a decisive majority. It has now been completed. The Senate about to assemble will also be Democratic. The offices of President and Vice-President have been put into the hands of Democrats. What does the change mean? That is the question that is uppermost in our minds to-day. That is the question I am going to try to answer, in order, if I may, to interpret the occasion.

It means much more than the mere success of a party. The success of a party means little except when the Nation is using that party for a large and definite purpose. No one can mistake the purpose for which the Nation now seeks to use the Democratic Party. It seeks to use it to interpret a change in its own plans and point of view. Some old things with which we had grown familiar, and which had begun to creep into the very habit of our thought and of our lives, have altered their aspect as we have latterly looked critically upon them, with fresh, awakened eyes; have dropped their disguises and shown themselves alien and sinister. Some new things, as we look frankly upon them, willing to comprehend their real character, have come to assume the aspect of things long believed in and familiar, stuff of our own convictions. We have been refreshed by a new insight into our own life.

We see that in many things that life is very great. It is incomparably great in its material aspects, in its body of wealth, in the diversity and sweep of its energy, in the industries which have been conceived and built up by the genius of individual men and the limitless enterprise of groups of men. It is great, also, very great, in its moral force. Nowhere else in the world have noble men and women exhibited in more striking forms the beauty and the energy of sympathy and helpfulness and counsel in their efforts to rectify wrong, alleviate suffering, and set the weak in the way of strength and hope. We have built up, moreover, a great system of government, which has stood through a long age as in many respects a model for those who seek to set liberty upon foundations that will endure against fortuitous change, against storm and accident. Our life contains every great thing, and contains it in rich abundance.

But the evil has come with the good, and much fine gold has been corroded. With riches has come inexcusable waste. We have squandered a great part of what we might have used, and have not stopped to conserve the exceeding bounty of nature, without which our genius for enterprise would have been worthless and impotent, scorning to be careful, shamefully prodigal as well as admirably efficient. We have been proud of our industrial achievements, but we have not hitherto stopped thoughtfully enough to count the human cost, the cost of lives snuffed out, of energies overtaxed and broken, the fearful physical and spiritual cost to the men and women and children upon whom the dead weight and burden of it all has fallen pitilessly the years through. The groans and agony of it all had not yet reached our ears, the solemn, moving undertone of our life, coming up out of the mines and factories, and out of every home where the struggle had its intimate and familiar seat. With the great Government went many deep secret things which we too long delayed to look into and scrutinize with candid, fearless eyes. The great Government we loved has too often been made use of for private and selfish purposes, and those who used it had forgotten the people.

At last a vision has been vouchsafed us of our life as a whole. We see the bad with the good, the debased and decadent with the sound and vital. With this vision we approach new affairs. Our duty is to cleanse, to reconsider, to restore, to correct the evil without impairing the good, to purify and humanize every process of our common life without weakening or sentimentalizing it. There has been something crude and heartless and unfeeling in our haste to succeed and be great. Our thought has been "Let every man look out for himself, let every generation look out for itself," while we reared giant machinery which made it impossible that any but those who stood at the levers of control should have a chance to look out for themselves. We had not forgotten our morals. We remembered well enough that we had set up a policy which was meant to serve the humblest as well as the most powerful, with an eye single to the standards of justice and fair play, and remembered it with pride. But we were very heedless and in a hurry to be great.

We have come now to the sober second thought. The scales of heedlessness have fallen from our eyes. We have made up our minds to square every process of our national life again with the standards we so proudly set up at the beginning and have always carried at our hearts. Our work is a work of restoration.

We have itemized with some degree of particularity the things that ought to be altered and here are some of the chief items: A tariff which cuts us off from our proper part in the commerce of the world, violates the just principles of taxation, and makes the Government a facile instrument in the hand of private interests; a banking and currency system based upon the necessity of the Government to sell its bonds fifty years ago and perfectly adapted to concentrating cash and restricting credits; an industrial system which, take it on all its sides, financial as well as administrative, holds capital in leading strings, restricts the liberties and limits the opportunities of labor, and exploits without renewing or conserving the natural resources of the country; a body of agricultural activities never yet given the efficiency of great business undertakings or served as it should be through the instrumentality of science taken directly to the farm, or afforded the facilities of credit best suited to its practical needs; watercourses undeveloped, waste places unreclaimed, forests untended, fast disappearing without plan or prospect of renewal, unregarded waste heaps at every mine. We have studied as perhaps no other nation has the most effective means of production, but we have not studied cost or economy as we should either as organizers of industry, as statesmen, or as individuals.

Nor have we studied and perfected the means by which government may be put at the service of humanity, in safeguarding the health of the Nation, the health of its men and its women and its children, as well as their rights in the struggle for existence. This is no sentimental duty. The firm basis of government is justice, not pity. These are matters of justice. There can be no equality or opportunity, the first essential of justice in the body politic, if men and women and children be not shielded in their lives, their very vitality, from the consequences of great industrial and social processes which they can not alter, control, or singly cope with. Society must see to it that it does not itself crush or weaken or damage its own constituent parts. The first duty of law is to keep sound the society it serves. Sanitary laws, pure food laws, and laws determining conditions of labor which individuals are powerless to determine for themselves are intimate parts of the very business of justice and legal efficiency.

These are some of the things we ought to do, and not leave the others undone, the old-fashioned, never-to-be-neglected, fundamental safeguarding of property and of individual right. This is the high enterprise of the new day: To lift everything that concerns our life as a Nation to the light that shines from the hearthfire of every man's conscience and vision of the right. It is inconceivable that we should do this as partisans; it is inconceivable we should do it in ignorance of the facts as they are or in blind haste. We shall restore, not destroy. We shall deal with our economic system as it is and as it may be modified, not as it might be if we had a clean sheet of paper to write upon; and step by step we shall make it what it should be, in the spirit of those who question their own wisdom and seek counsel and knowledge, not shallow self-satisfaction or the excitement of excursions whither they can not tell. Justice, and only justice, shall always be our motto.

And yet it will be no cool process of mere science. The Nation has been deeply stirred, stirred by a solemn passion, stirred by the knowledge of wrong, of ideals lost, of government too often debauched and made an instrument of evil. The feelings with which we face this new age of right and opportunity sweep across our heartstrings like some air out of God's own presence, where justice and mercy are reconciled and the judge and the brother are one. We

Menu card for inaugural evening dinner given by Wilson's 1879 Princeton classmates. The tiger is Princeton's symbol.

At first, Wilson planned to center his presidential campaign on the tariff. But, he soon realized that this was a worn-out issue. On August 28, 1912, he met Louis D. Brandeis for the first time. Brandeis was the chief spokesman of the philosophy of regulated competition and economic freedom for the small businessman. It was Brandeis who influenced Wilson's thought and led him to believe that the most vital question confronting the American people was the preservation of economic freedom. Wilson explained this in his campaign speeches—business had to be set free from the shackles of monopoly. While Roosevelt claimed that the great corporations were often the most efficient units of industrial organization and that they should be regulated by a powerful federal trade commission, Wilson envisioned clearing the economic market of monopolistic obstructions. "Theirs," Wilson declared, "is a program of regulation, while ours is a program of liberty."

know our task to be no mere task of politics but a task which shall search us through and through, whether we be able to understand our time and the need of our people, whether we be indeed their spokesmen and interpreters, whether we have the pure heart to comprehend and the rectified will to choose our high course of action.

This is not a day of triumph; it is a day of dedication. Here muster, not the forces of party, but the forces of humanity. Men's hearts wait upon us; men's lives hang in the balance; men's hopes call upon us to say what we will do. Who shall live up to the great trust? Who dares fail to try? I summon all honest men, all patriotic, all forward-looking men, to my side. God helping me, I will not fail them, if they will but counsel and sustain me!

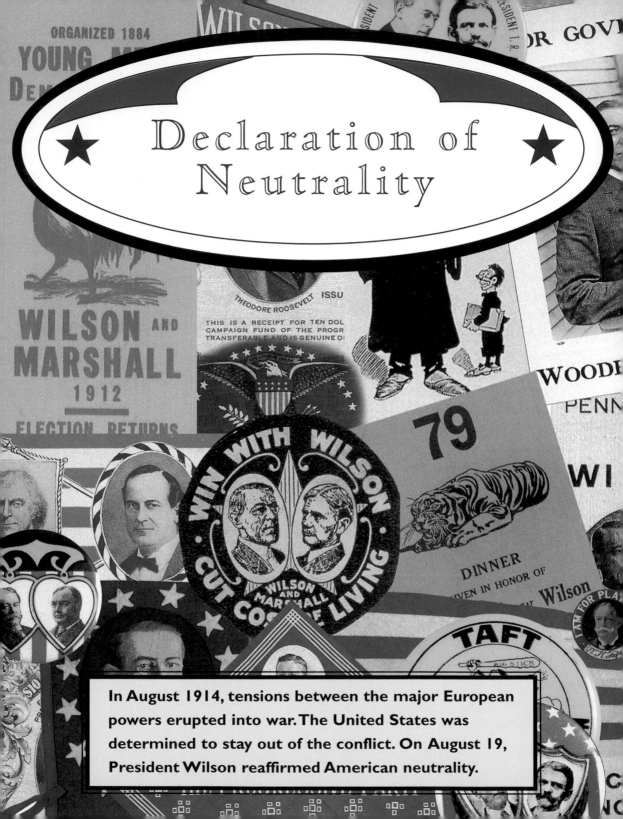

Declaration of Neutrality

In August 1914, tensions between the major European powers erupted into war. The United States was determined to stay out of the conflict. On August 19, President Wilson reaffirmed American neutrality.

The effect of the war upon the United States will depend upon what American citizens say and do. Every man who really loves America will act and speak in the true spirit of neutrality, which is the spirit of impartiality and fairness and friendliness to all concerned. The spirit of the nation in this critical matter will be determined largely by what individuals and society and those gathered in public meetings do and say, upon what newspapers and magazines contain, upon what ministers utter in their pulpits, and men proclaim as their opinions upon the street.

The people of the United States are drawn from many nations, and chiefly from the nations now at war. It is natural and inevitable that there should be the utmost variety of sympathy and desire among them with regard to the issues and circumstances of the conflict. Some will wish one nation, others another, to succeed in the momentous struggle. It will be easy to excite passion and difficult to allay it. Those responsible for exciting it will assume a heavy responsibility, responsibility for no less a thing than that the people of the United States, whose love of their country and whose loyalty to its government should unite them as Americans all, bound in honor and affection to think first of her and her interests, may be divided in camps of hostile opinion, hot against each other, involved in the war itself in impulse and opinion if not in action.

Such divisions amongst us would be fatal to our peace of mind and might seriously stand in the way of the proper performance of our duty as the one great nation at peace, the one people holding itself ready to play a part of impartial mediation and speak the counsels of peace and accommodation, not as a partisan, but as a friend.

I venture, therefore, my fellow countrymen, to speak a solemn word of warning to you against that deepest, most subtle, most essential breach of neutrality which may spring out of partisanship, out of passionately taking sides. The United States must be neutral in fact, as well as in name, during these days that are to try men's souls. We must be impartial in thought, as well as action, must put a curb upon our sentiments, as well as upon every transaction that might be construed as a preference of one party to the struggle before another.

Wilson's talent for leadership, combined with the progressive temper of the times, resulted in an amazing spurt of legislation. This adroit chief executive had established his firm control over both Congress and the Democratic Party. Tariff reductions, banking reforms, stronger antimonopoly legislation, assistance to agriculture, and conservation legislation—the major progressive demands—had been enacted into law. Wilson thought the New Freedom legislation had righted fundamental wrongs. Although more advanced progressives questioned whether Wilson understood the far-reaching social and economic tensions of the day, there can be no doubt that his first administration represents the climax of an era of reform and the end of an era of peace.

Outbreak of war in Europe in August 1914 stunned Americans. Europe had been on the brink of conflict for more than a decade, but when the clash came most Americans were shocked at the thought of organized slaughter. On August 19, Wilson appealed to the nation to remain impartial in thought, as well as in action. Nevertheless, sentiment against Germany grew. The President himself, an ardent admirer of the British parliamentary system, privately confided as early as August 30, 1914, that "if Germany wins, it will change the course of our civilization, and make the United States a military nation." Both the American people and the administration, however, desired neutrality. Throughout 1915 and 1916, the President, his patience often frayed by provoking British and German incidents, attempted to follow this course.

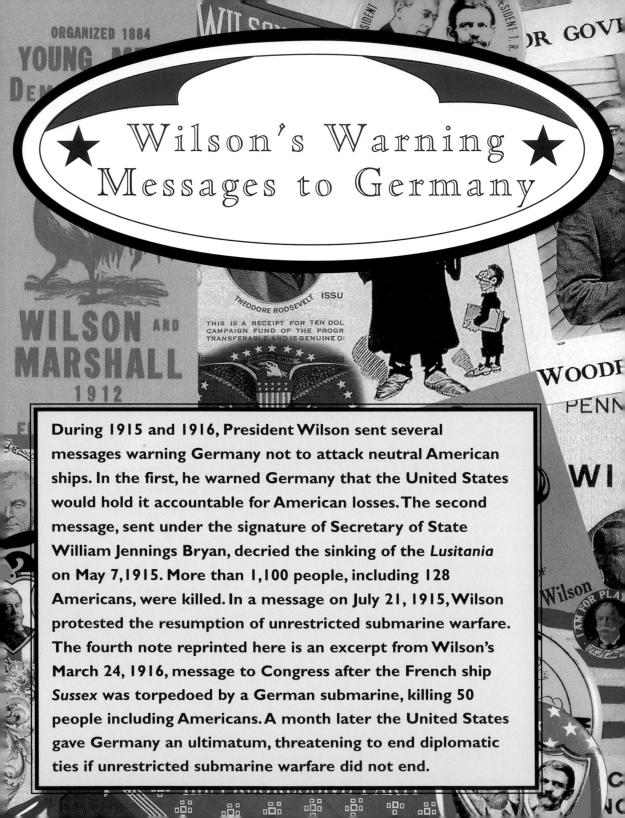

★ Wilson's Warning Messages to Germany ★

During 1915 and 1916, President Wilson sent several messages warning Germany not to attack neutral American ships. In the first, he warned Germany that the United States would hold it accountable for American losses. The second message, sent under the signature of Secretary of State William Jennings Bryan, decried the sinking of the *Lusitania* on May 7, 1915. More than 1,100 people, including 128 Americans, were killed. In a message on July 21, 1915, Wilson protested the resumption of unrestricted submarine warfare. The fourth note reprinted here is an excerpt from Wilson's March 24, 1916, message to Congress after the French ship *Sussex* was torpedoed by a German submarine, killing 50 people including Americans. A month later the United States gave Germany an ultimatum, threatening to end diplomatic ties if unrestricted submarine warfare did not end.

First Message, February 10, 1915

The Government of the United State views those possibilities with such grave concern that it feels it to be its privilege, and, indeed, its duty, in the circumstances, to request the Imperial German Government to consider, before action is taken, the critical situation in respect of the relation between this country and Germany—which might arise were the German naval force, in carrying out the policy foreshadowed in the Admiralty's proclamation, to destroy any merchant vessel of the United States or cause the death of American citizens.

It is, of course, not necessary to remind the German Government that the sole right of a belligerent in dealing with neutral vessels on the high seas is limited to visit and search, unless a blockade is proclaimed and effectively maintained, which this Government does not understand to be proposed in this case. To declare or exercise a right to attack and destroy any vessel entering a prescribed area of the high seas without first certainly determining its belligerent nationality and the contraband character of its cargo would be an act so unprecedented in naval warfare that this government is reluctant to believe that the Imperial Government of Germany in this case contemplates it as possible.

The suspicion that enemy ships are using neutral flags improperly can create no just presumption that all ships traversing a prescribed area are subject to the same suspicion. It is to determine exactly such questions that this Government understands the right of visit and search to have been recognized.

This Government has carefully noted the explanatory statement issued by the Imperial German Government at the same time with the proclamation of the German Admiralty, and takes this occasion to remind the Imperial German Government very respectfully that the Government of the United States is open to none of the criticisms for unneutral action to which the German Government believes the governments of certain other neutral nations have laid themselves open; that the Government of the United State has not consented to or acquiesced in any measures which may have been taken by the other belligerent nations in the present war which operate to restrain neutral trade, but has, on the contrary, taken in all such matters a position which warrants it in holding those governments responsible in the proper way for any untoward effects on American shipping which the accepted principles of international law do not justify; and that it, therefore, regards itself as free in the present instance to take with a clear conscience and upon accepted principles the position indicated in this note.

If the commanders of German vessels of war should act upon the presumption that the flag of the United States was not being used in good faith and should destroy on the high seas an American vessel or the lives of American citizens, it would be difficult for the Government of the United States to view the act in any other light than as an indefensible violation of neutral rights, which it would be very hard, indeed, to reconcile with the friendly relations now happily subsisting between the two governments.

If such a deplorable situation should arise, the Imperial German Government can readily appreciate that the Government of the United States would be constrained to hold the Imperial Government of Germany to a strict accountability for such acts of their naval authorities, and to take any steps it might be necessary to take to safeguard American lives and property and to secure to American citizens the full enjoyment of their acknowledged rights on the high seas.

The Government of the United States, in view of these considerations, which it urges with the sincere purpose of making sure that no misunderstandings may arise, and no circumstances occur, that might even cloud the intercourse of the two governments, expresses the confident hope and expectation that the Imperial German Government can and will give assurance that American citizens and their vessels will not be molested by the naval forces of

Germany otherwise than by visit and search, though their vessels may be traversing the sea area delimited in the proclamation of the German Admiralty.

It is stated for the information of the Imperial Government that representations have been made to his Britannic Majesty's Government in respect to the unwarranted use of the American flag for the protection of British ships.

The *Lusitania* Note, May 13, 1915

In view of recent acts of the German authorities in violation of American rights on the high seas which culminated in the torpedoing and sinking of the British steamship *Lusitania* on May 7, 1915, by which over 100 American citizens lost their lives, it is clearly wise and desirable that the Government of the United States and the Imperial German Government should come to a clear and full understanding as to the grave situation which has resulted.

The sinking of the British passenger steamer *Falaba* by a German submarine on March 28, through which Leon C. Thrasher, an American citizen, was drowned; the attack on April 28 on the American vessel *Cushing* by a German aeroplane; the torpedoing on May 1 of the American vessel *Gulflight* by a German submarine, as a result of which two or more American citizens met their death and, finally, the torpedoing and sinking of the steamship *Lusitania*, constitute a series of events which the Government of the United States has observed with growing concern, distress, and amazement.

Recalling the humane and enlightened attitude hitherto assumed by the Imperial German Government in matters of international right, and particularly with regard to the freedom of the seas; having learned to recognize the German views and the German influence in the field of international obligation as always engaged upon the side of justice and humanity; and having understood the instructions of the Imperial German Government to its naval commanders to be upon the same plane of human action prescribed by the naval codes of other nations, the Government of the United States was loath to believe—it cannot now bring itself to believe—that these acts, so absolutely contrary to the rules, the practices, and the spirit of modern warfare, could have the countenance or sanction of that great Government. It feels it to be its duty, therefore, to address the Imperial German Government concerning them with the utmost frankness and in the earnest hope that it is not mistaken in expecting action on the part of the Imperial German Government which will correct the unfortunate impressions which have been created and vindicate once more the position of that Government with regard to the sacred freedom of the seas.

The Government of the United States has been apprised that the Imperial German Government considered themselves to be obliged by the extraordinary circumstances of the present war and the measures adopted by their adversaries in seeking to cut Germany off from all commerce, to adopt methods of retaliation which go much beyond the ordinary methods of warfare at sea, in the proclamation of a war zone from which they have warned neutral ships to keep away. This Government has already taken occasion to inform the Imperial German Government that it cannot admit the adoption of such measures or such a warning of danger to operate as in any degree an abbreviation of the rights of American shipmasters or of American citizens bound on lawful errands as passengers on merchant ships of belligerent nationality; and that it must hold the Imperial German Government to a strict accountability for any infringement of those rights, intentional or incidental. [. . .]

The Government of the United States, therefore, desires to call the attention of the Imperial German Government with the utmost earnestness to the fact that the objection to their present method of attack against the trade of their enemies lies in the practical impossibility of employing submarines in the destruction of commerce without disregarding those rules of fairness, reason, justice, and humanity, which all modern opinion regards as imperative. [. . .] The Government and the people of the United States look to the Imperial German Government for just, prompt, and enlightened action in this vital matter with the greater confidence because the United States and Germany are bound together not only for special ties of friendship but also by the explicit stipulations of the treaty of 1828 between the United States and the Kingdom of Prussia.

Expressions of regret and offers of reparation in case of the destruction of neutral ships sunk by mistake, while they may satisfy international obligations, if no loss of life results, cannot justify or excuse a practice, the natural and necessary effect of which is to subject neutral nations and neutral persons to new and immeasurable risks.

The Imperial German Government will not expect the Government of the United States to omit any word or any act necessary to the performance of its sacred duty of maintaining the rights of the United States and its citizens and of safeguarding their free exercise and enjoyment.

Wilson's Protest, July 21, 1915

The Government of the United States is not unmindful of the extraordinary conditions created by this war [. . .] and it is ready to make every reasonable allowance for these novel and unexpected aspects of war at sea; but it can not consent to abate any essential or fundamental right of its people because of a mere alteration of circumstance. The rights of neutrals in time of war are based upon principle, not upon expediency, and the principles are immutable. It is the duty and obligation of belligerents to find a way to adapt the new circumstances to them.

The events of the past two months have clearly indicated that it is possible and practicable to conduct such submarine operations as have characterized the activity of the Imperial German Navy within the so-called war zone in substantial accord with the accepted practices of regulated warfare. The whole world has looked with interest and increasing satisfaction at the demonstration of that possibility by German naval commanders. It is manifestly possible, therefore, to lift the whole practice of submarine attack above the criticism which it has aroused and remove the chief causes of offense.

In view of the admission of illegality made by the Imperial Government when it pleaded the right of retaliation in defense of its acts, and in view of the manifest possibility of conforming to the established rules of naval warfare, the Government of the United States can not believe that the Imperial Government will longer refrain from disavowing the wanton act of its naval commander in sinking the *Lusitania* or from offering reparation for the American lives lost, so far as reparation can be made for a needless destruction of human life by an illegal act.

The Government of the United States, while not indifferent to the friendly spirit in which it is made, can not accept the suggestion of the Imperial German Government that certain vessels be designated and agreed upon which shall be free on the seas now illegally proscribed. The very agreement would, by implication, subject other vessels to illegal attack, and would be a curtailment and therefore an abandonment of the principles for which this government contends, and which in times of calmer counsels every nation would concede as of course. The Government of the United States and the Imperial German Government are contending for the same great object, have long stood together in urging the very principles upon which the Government of the United States now so solemnly insists. They are both contending for the freedom of the seas.

The Government of the United States will continue to contend for that freedom, from whatever quarter violated. without compromise and at any cost. It invites the practical cooperation of the Imperial German Government at this time, when cooperation may accomplish most and this great common object be most strikingly and effectively achieved. [. . .] Repetition by the commanders of German naval vessels of acts in contravention of those [neutral] rights must be regarded by the Government of the United States, when they affect American citizens, as deliberately unfriendly.

Wilson on the *Sussex* incident, April 19, 1916

[. . .] I have deemed it my duty, therefore, to say to the Imperial German Government, that if it is still its purpose to prosecute relentless and indiscriminate warfare against vessels of commerce by the use of submarines, notwithstanding the now demonstrated impossibility of conducting that warfare in accordance with what the Government of the United States must consider the sacred and indisputable rules of international law and the universally recognized dictates of humanity, the Government of the United States is at last forced to the conclusion that there is but one course it can pursue; and that unless the Imperial German Government should now immediately declare and effect an abandonment of its present methods of warfare against passenger and freight carrying vessels this Government can have no choice but to sever diplomatic relations with the Government of the German Empire altogether.

This decision I have arrived at with the keenest regret; the possibility of the action contemplated I am sure all thoughtful Americans will look forward to with unaffected reluctance. But we cannot forget that we are in some sort and by the force of circumstances the responsible spokesmen of the rights of humanity, and that we cannot remain silent while those rights seem in process of being swept utterly away in the maelstrom of this terrible war. We owe it to a due regard to our own rights as a nation, to our sense of duty as a representative of the rights of neutrals the world over, and to a just conception of the rights of mankind to take this stand now with the utmost solemnity and firmness. [. . .]

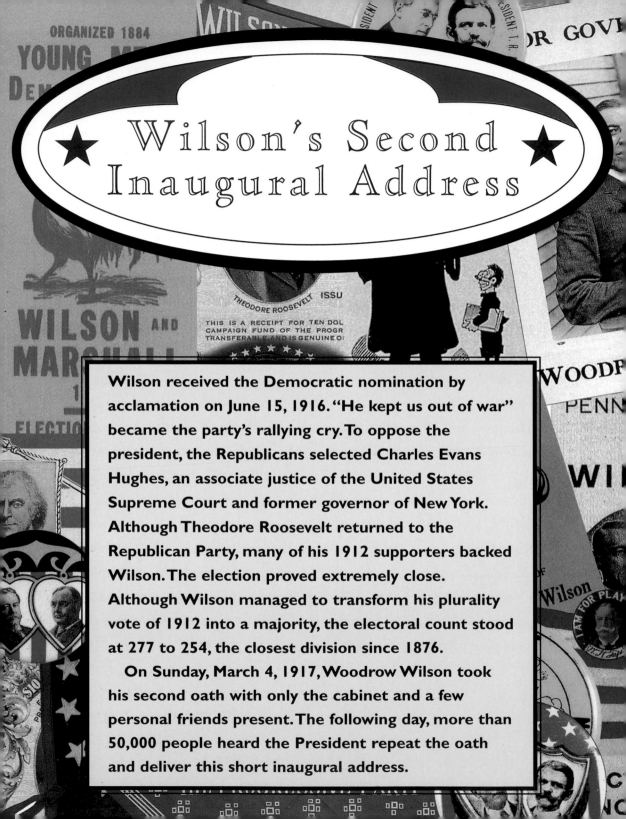

★ Wilson's Second Inaugural Address ★

Wilson received the Democratic nomination by acclamation on June 15, 1916. "He kept us out of war" became the party's rallying cry. To oppose the president, the Republicans selected Charles Evans Hughes, an associate justice of the United States Supreme Court and former governor of New York. Although Theodore Roosevelt returned to the Republican Party, many of his 1912 supporters backed Wilson. The election proved extremely close. Although Wilson managed to transform his plurality vote of 1912 into a majority, the electoral count stood at 277 to 254, the closest division since 1876.

On Sunday, March 4, 1917, Woodrow Wilson took his second oath with only the cabinet and a few personal friends present. The following day, more than 50,000 people heard the President repeat the oath and deliver this short inaugural address.

The four years which have elapsed since last I stood in this place have been crowded with counsel and action of the most vital interest and consequence. Perhaps no equal period in our history has been so fruitful of important reforms in our economic and industrial life or so full of significant changes in the spirit and purpose of our political action. We have sought very thoughtfully to set our house in order, correct the grosser errors and abuses of our industrial life, liberate and quicken the processes of our national genius and energy, and lift our politics to a broader view of the people's essential interests.

It is a record of singular variety and singular distinction. But I shall not attempt to review it. It speaks for itself and will be of increasing influence as the years go by. This is not the time for retrospect. It is time rather to speak our thoughts and purposes concerning the present and the immediate future.

Although we have centered counsel and action with such unusual concentration and success upon the great problems of domestic legislation to which we addressed ourselves four years ago, other matters have more and more forced themselves upon our attention—matters lying outside our own life as a nation and over which we had no control, but which, despite our wish to keep free of them, have drawn us more and more irresistibly into their own current and influence.

It has been impossible to avoid them. They have affected the life of the whole world. They have shaken men everywhere with a passion and an apprehension they never knew before. It has been hard to preserve calm counsel while the thought of our own people swayed this way and that under their influence. We are a composite and cosmopolitan people. We are of the blood of all the nations that are at war. The currents of our thoughts as well as the currents of our trade run quick at all seasons back and forth between us and them. The war inevitably set its mark from the first alike upon our minds, our industries, our commerce, our politics and our social action. To be indifferent to it, or independent of it, was out of the question.

And yet all the while we have been conscious that we were not part of it. In that consciousness, despite many divisions, we have drawn closer together. We have been deeply wronged upon the seas, but we have not wished to wrong or injure in return; have retained throughout the consciousness of standing in some sort apart, intent upon an interest that transcended the immediate issues of the war itself.

As some of the injuries done us have become intolerable we have still been clear that we wished nothing for ourselves that we were not ready to demand for all mankind—fair dealing, justice, the freedom to live and to be at ease against organized wrong.

It is in this spirit and with this thought that we have grown more and more aware, more and more certain that the part we wished to play was the part of those who mean to vindicate and fortify peace. We have been obliged to arm ourselves to make good our claim to a certain minimum of right and of freedom of action. We stand firm in armed neutrality since it seems that in no other way we can demonstrate what it is we insist upon and cannot forget. We may even be drawn on, by circumstances, not by our own purpose or desire, to a more active assertion of our rights as we see them and a more immediate association with the great struggle itself. But nothing will alter our thought or our purpose. They are too clear to be obscured. They are too deeply rooted in the principles of our national life to be altered. We desire neither conquest nor advantage. We wish nothing that can be had only at the cost of another people. We always professed unselfish purpose and we covet the opportunity to prove our professions are sincere.

There are many things still to be done at home, to clarify our own politics and add new vitality to the industrial processes of our own life, and we shall do them as time and opportunity serve, but we realize that the greatest things

Wilson, as president, supported women's suffrage. The Nineteenth Amendment, ratified in August 1920 during the waning months of his second administration, gave women the right to vote.

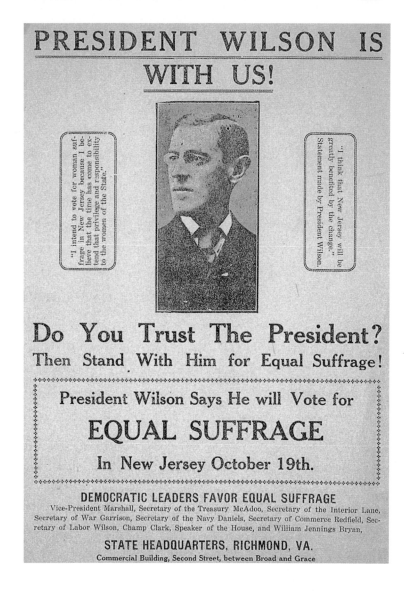

PRESIDENT WILSON IS WITH US!

"I intend to vote for woman suffrage in New Jersey because I believe that the time has come to extend that privilege and responsibility to the women of the State."

"I think that New Jersey will be greatly benefited by the change." Statement made by President Wilson.

Do You Trust The President?
Then Stand With Him for Equal Suffrage!

President Wilson Says He will Vote for

EQUAL SUFFRAGE

In New Jersey October 19th.

DEMOCRATIC LEADERS FAVOR EQUAL SUFFRAGE
Vice-President Marshall, Secretary of the Treasury McAdoo, Secretary of the Interior Lane, Secretary of War Garrison, Secretary of the Navy Daniels, Secretary of Commerce Redfield, Secretary of Labor Wilson, Champ Clark, Speaker of the House, and William Jennings Bryan,

STATE HEADQUARTERS, RICHMOND, VA.
Commercial Building, Second Street, between Broad and Grace

that remain to be done must be done with the whole world for stage and in cooperation with the wide and universal forces of mankind, and we are making our spirits ready for those things.

We are provincials no longer. The tragic events of the thirty months of vital turmoil through which we have just passed have made us citizens of the world. There can be no turning back. Our own fortunes as a nation are involved whether we would have it so or not.

And yet we are not the less Americans on that account. We shall be the more American if we but remain true to the principles in which we have been bred. They are not the principles of a province or of a single continent. We have known and boasted all along that they were the principles of a liberated mankind. These, therefore, are the things we shall stand for, whether in war or in peace:

That all nations are equally interested in the peace of the world and in the political stability of free peoples, and equally responsible for their maintenance; that the essential principle of peace is the actual equality of nations in all matters of right or privilege; that peace cannot securely or justly rest upon an armed balance of power; that governments derive all their just powers from the consent of the governed and that no other powers should be supported by the common thought, purpose or power of the family of nations; that the seas should be equally free and safe for the use of all peoples, under rules set up by common agreement and consent, and that, so far as practicable, they should be accessible to all upon equal terms; that national armaments shall be limited to the necessities of national order and domestic safety; that the community of interest and of power upon which peace must henceforth depend imposes upon each nation the duty of seeing to it that all influences proceeding from its own citizens meant to encourage or assist revolution in other states should be sternly and effectually suppressed and prevented.

I need not argue these principles to you, my fellow countrymen; they are your own part and parcel of your own thinking and your own motives in affairs. They spring up native amongst us. Upon this as a platform of purpose and of action we can stand together. And it is imperative that we should stand together. We are being forged into a new unity amidst the fires that now blaze throughout the world. In their ardent heat we shall, in God's Providence, let us hope, be purged of faction and division, purified of the errant humors of party and of private interest, and shall stand forth in the days to come with a new dignity of national pride and spirit. Let each man see to it that the dedication is in his own heart, the high purpose of the nation in his own mind, ruler of his own will and desire.

I stand here and have taken the high and solemn oath to which you have been audience because the people of the United States have chosen me for this august delegation of power and have by their gracious judgment named me their leader in affairs.

I know now what the task means. I realize to the full the responsibility which it involves. I pray God I may be given the wisdom and the prudence to do my duty in the true spirit of this great people. I am their servant and can succeed only as they sustain and guide me by their confidence and their counsel. The thing I shall count upon, the thing without which neither counsel nor action will avail, is the unity of America—an America united in feeling, in purpose and in its vision of duty, of opportunity and of service.

We are to beware of all men who would turn the tasks and the necessities of the nation to their own private profit or use them for the building up of private power.

United alike in the conception of our duty and in the high resolve to perform it in the face of all men, let us dedicate ourselves to the great task to which we must now set our hand. For myself I beg your tolerance, your countenance and your united aid.

The shadows that now lie dark upon our path will soon be dispelled, and we shall walk with the light all about us if we be but true to ourselves—to ourselves as we have wished to be known in the counsels of the world and in the thought of all those who love liberty and justice and the right exalted.

Wilson's War Message

On February 3, 1917, the United States severed diplomatic relations with Germany. Three weeks later, British intelligence gave the United States an alleged telegram from the German foreign secretary, Alfred Zimmerman, to the German ambassador in Mexico, suggesting an alliance between Mexico and Germany if the U.S. entered the war against Germany. Mexico would recover its "lost territories"—Texas, Arizona, and New Mexico. On April 2, 1917, in a special session of Congress, President Wilson delivered this "War Message." Four days later, Congress voted to declare war on Germany.

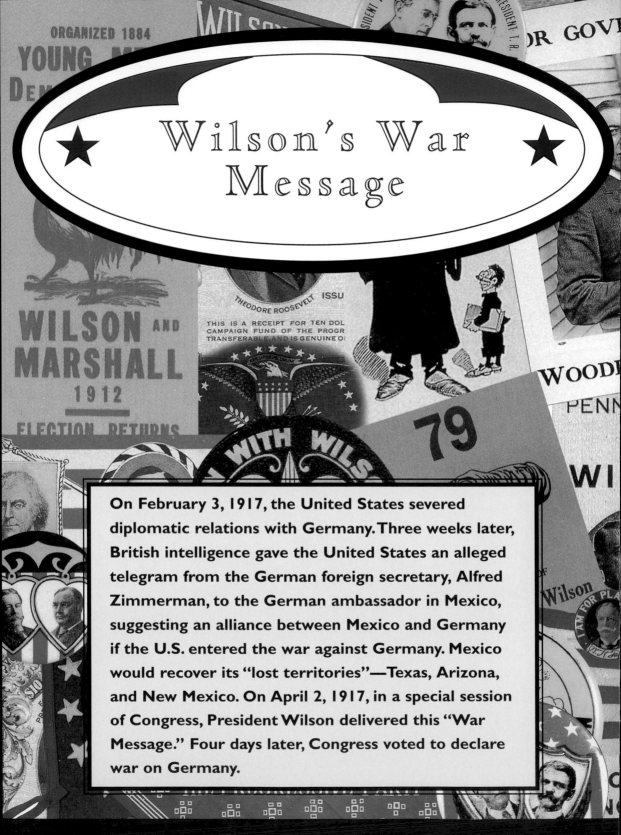

I have called the Congress into extraordinary session because there are serious, very serious, choices of policy to be made, and made immediately, which it was neither right nor constitutionally permissible that I should assume the responsibility of making.

On the 3d of February last I officially laid before you the extraordinary announcement of the Imperial German Government that on and after the 1st day of February it was its purpose to put aside all restraints of law or of humanity and use its submarines to sink every vessel that sought to approach either the ports of Great Britain and Ireland or the western coasts of Europe or any of the ports controlled by the enemies of Germany within the Mediterranean. That had seemed to be the object of the German submarine warfare earlier in the war, but since April of last year the Imperial Government had somewhat restrained the commanders of its undersea craft in conformity with its promise then given to us that passenger boats should not be sunk and that due warning would be given to all other vessels which its submarines might seek to destroy, when no resistance was offered or escape attempted, and care taken that their crews were given at least a fair chance to save their lives in their open boats. The precautions taken were meagre and haphazard enough, as was proved in distressing instance after instance in the progress of the cruel and unmanly business, but a certain degree of restraint was observed.

The new policy has swept every restriction aside. Vessels of every kind, whatever their flag, their character, their cargo, their destination, their errand, have been ruthlessly sent to the bottom without warning and without thought of help or mercy for those on board, the vessels of friendly neutrals along with those of belligerents. Even hospital ships and ships carrying relief to the sorely bereaved and stricken people of Belgium, though the latter were provided with safe-conduct through the proscribed areas by the German Government itself and were distinguished by unmistakable marks of identity, have been sunk with the same reckless lack of compassion or of principle.

I was for a little while unable to believe that such things would in fact be done by any government that had hitherto subscribed to the humane practices of civilized nations. International law had its origin in the attempt to set up some law which would be respected and observed upon the seas, where no nation had right of dominion and where lay the free highways of the world. By painful stage after stage has that law been built up, with meagre enough results, indeed, after all was accomplished that could be accomplished, but always with a clear view, at least, of what the heart and conscience of mankind demanded. This minimum of right the German Government has swept aside under the plea of retaliation and necessity and because it had no weapons which it could use at sea except these which it is impossible to employ as it is employing them without throwing to the winds all scruples of humanity or of respect for the understandings that were supposed to underlie the intercourse of the world. I am not now thinking of the loss of property involved, immense and serious as that is, but only of the wanton and wholesale destruction of the lives of noncombatants, men, women, and children, engaged in pursuits which have always, even in the darkest periods of modern history, been deemed innocent and legitimate. Property can be paid for; the lives of peaceful and innocent people can not be. The present German submarine warfare against commerce is a warfare against mankind.

It is a war against all nations. American ships have been sunk, American lives taken, in ways which it has stirred us very deeply to learn of, but the ships and people of other neutral and friendly nations have been sunk and overwhelmed in the waters in the same way. There has been no discrimination. The challenge is to all mankind. Each nation must decide for itself how it will meet it. The choice we make for ourselves must be made with a moderation of counsel and a temperateness of judgment befitting our character and our motives as a nation. We must put excited feeling away. Our motive will not be revenge or the victorious assertion of the physical might of the nation, but only the vindication of right, of human right, of which we are only a single champion.

When I addressed the Congress on the 26th of February last, I thought that it would suffice to assert our neutral rights with arms, our right to use the seas against unlawful interference, our right to keep our people safe against unlawful violence. But armed neutrality, it now appears, is impracticable. Because submarines are in effect outlaws when used as the German submarines have been used against merchant shipping, it is impossible to defend ships against their attacks as the law of nations has assumed that merchantmen would defend themselves against privateers or cruisers, visible craft giving chase upon the open sea. It is common prudence in such circumstances, grim necessity indeed, to endeavour to destroy them before they have shown their own intention. They must be dealt with upon sight, if dealt with at all. The German Government denies the right of neutrals to use arms at all within the areas of the sea which it has proscribed, even in the defense of rights which no modern publicist has ever before questioned their right to defend. The intimation is conveyed that the armed guards which we have placed on our merchant ships will be treated as beyond the pale of law and subject to be dealt with as pirates would be. Armed neutrality is ineffectual enough at best; in such circumstances and in the face of such pretensions it is worse than ineffectual; it is likely only to produce what it was meant to prevent; it is practically certain to draw us into the war without either the rights or the effectiveness of belligerents. There is one choice we can not make, we are incapable of making: we will not choose the path of submission and suffer the most sacred rights of our nation and our people to be ignored or violated. The wrongs against which we now array ourselves are no common wrongs; they cut to the very roots of human life.

With a profound sense of the solemn and even tragical character of the step I am taking and of the grave responsibilities which it involves, but in unhesitating obedience to what I deem my constitutional duty, I advise that the Congress declare the recent course of the Imperial German Government to be in fact nothing less than war against the Government and people of the United States; that it formally accept the status of belligerent which has thus been thrust upon it, and that it take immediate steps not only to put the country in a more thorough state of defense but also to exert all its power and employ all its resources to bring the Government of the German Empire to terms and end the war.

What this will involve is clear. It will involve the utmost practicable cooperation in counsel and action with the governments now at war with Germany, and, as incident to that, the extension to those governments of the most liberal financial credits, in order that our resources may so far as possible be added to theirs. It will involve the organization and mobilization of all the material resources of the country to supply the materials of war and serve the incidental needs of the nation in the most abundant and yet the most economical and efficient way possible. It will involve the immediate full equipment of the Navy in all respects but particularly in supplying it with the best means of dealing with the enemy's submarines. It will involve the immediate addition to the armed forces of the United States already provided for by law in case of war at least 500,000 men, who should, in my opinion, be chosen upon the principle of universal liability to service, and also the authorization of subsequent additional increments of equal force so soon as they may be needed and can be handled in training. It will involve also, of course, the granting of adequate credits to the Government, sustained, I hope, so far as they can equitably be sustained by the present generation, by well conceived taxation. [. . .]

While we do these things, these deeply momentous things, let us be very clear, and make very clear to all the world what our motives and our objects are. My own thought has not been driven from its habitual and normal course by the unhappy events of the last two months, and I do not believe that the thought of the nation has been altered or clouded by them I have exactly the same things in mind now that I had in mind when I addressed the Senate on the 22d of January last; the same that I had in mind when I addressed the Congress on the 3d of February and on the 26th of February. Our object now, as then, is to vindicate the principles of peace and justice in the life of the world as against selfish and autocratic power and to set up amongst the really free and self-governed peoples of the world such a concert of purpose and of action as will henceforth ensure the observance of those principles. Neutrality is no longer feasible or desirable where the peace of the world is involved and the freedom of its peoples, and the menace to that peace and freedom lies in the existence of autocratic governments backed by organized force which is controlled wholly by their will, not by the will of their people. We have seen the last of neutrality in such circumstances. We are at the beginning of an age in which it will be insisted that the same standards of conduct and of responsibility for wrong done shall be observed among nations and their governments that are observed among the individual citizens of civilized states.

We have no quarrel with the German people. We have no feeling towards them but one of sympathy and friendship. It was not upon their impulse that their Government acted in entering this war. It was not with their previous knowledge or approval. It was a war determined upon as wars used to be determined upon in the old, unhappy days when peoples were nowhere consulted by their rulers and wars were provoked and waged in the interest of dynasties or of little groups of ambitious men who were accustomed to use their fellow men as pawns and tools. Self-governed nations do not fill their neighbour states with spies or set the course of intrigue to bring about some critical posture of affairs which will give them an opportunity to strike and make conquest. Such designs can be successfully worked out only under cover and where no one has the right to ask questions. Cunningly contrived plans of deception or aggression, carried, it may be, from generation to generation, can be worked out and kept from the light only within the privacy of courts or behind the carefully guarded confidences of a narrow and privileged class.

They are happily impossible where public opinion commands and insists upon full information concerning all the nation's affairs.

A steadfast concert for peace can never be maintained except by a partnership of democratic nations. No autocratic government could be trusted to keep faith within it or observe its covenants. It must be a league of honour, a partnership of opinion. Intrigue would eat its vitals away; the plottings of inner circles who could plan what they would and render account to no one would be a corruption seated at its very heart. Only free peoples can hold their purpose and their honour steady to a common end and prefer the interests of mankind to any narrow interest of their own.

Does not every American feel that assurance has been added to our hope for the future peace of the world by the wonderful and heartening things that have been happening within the last few weeks in Russia? Russia was known by those who knew it best to have been always in fact democratic at heart, in all the vital habits of her thought, in all the intimate relationships of her people that spoke their natural instinct, their habitual attitude towards life. The autocracy that crowned the summit of her political structure, long as it had stood and terrible as was the reality of its power, was not in fact Russian in origin, character, or purpose; and now it has been shaken off and the great, generous Russian people have been added in all their naive majesty and might to the forces that are fighting for freedom in the world, for justice, and for peace. Here is a fit partner for a league of honour.

One of the things that has served to convince us that the Prussian autocracy was not and could never be our friend is that from the very outset of the present war it has filled our unsuspecting communities and even our offices of government with spies and set criminal intrigues everywhere afoot against our national unity of counsel, our peace within and without our industries and our commerce. Indeed it is now evident that its spies were here even before the war began; and it is unhappily not a matter of conjecture but a fact proved in our courts of justice that the intrigues which have more than once come perilously near to disturbing the peace and dislocating the industries of the country have been carried on at the instigation, with the support, and even under the personal direction of official agents of the Imperial Government accredited to the Government of the United States. Even in checking these things and trying to extirpate them we have sought to put the most generous interpretation possible upon them because we knew that their source lay, not in any hostile feeling or purpose of the German people towards us (who were, no doubt, as ignorant of them as we ourselves were), but only in the selfish designs of a Government that did what it pleased and told its people nothing. But they have played their part in serving to convince us at last that that Government entertains no real friendship for us and means to act against our peace and security at its convenience. That it means to stir up enemies against us at our very doors the intercepted [Zimmermann] note to the German Minister at Mexico City is eloquent evidence.

We are accepting this challenge of hostile purpose because we know that in such a government, following such methods, we can never have a friend; and that in the presence of its organized power, always lying in wait to accomplish we know not what purpose, there can be no assured security for the democratic governments of the world. We are now about to accept gage of battle with this natural foe to liberty and shall, if necessary, spend the whole force of the nation to check and nullify its pretensions and its power. We are glad, now that we see the facts with no veil of false pretense about them, to fight thus for the ultimate peace of the world and for the liberation of its peoples, the German peoples included: for the rights of nations great and small and the privilege of men everywhere to choose their way of life and of obedience. The world must be made safe for democracy. Its peace must be planted upon the tested foundations of political liberty. We have no selfish ends to serve. We desire no conquest, no dominion. We seek no indemnities for ourselves, no material compensation for the sacrifices we shall freely make. We are but one of the champions of the rights of mankind. We shall be satisfied when those rights have been made as secure as the faith and the freedom of nations can make them.

Just because we fight without rancour and without selfish object, seeking nothing for ourselves but what we shall wish to share with all free peoples, we shall, I feel confident, conduct our operations as belligerents without passion and ourselves observe with proud punctilio the principles of right and of fair play we profess to be fighting for.

I have said nothing of the governments allied with the Imperial Government of Germany because they have not made war upon us or challenged us to defend our right and our honour. The Austro-Hungarian Government has, indeed, avowed its unqualified endorsement and acceptance of the reckless and lawless submarine warfare adopted now without disguise by the Imperial German Government, and it has therefore not been possible for this Government to receive Count Tarnowski, the Ambassador recently accredited to this Government by the Imperial and Royal Government of Austria-Hungary; but that Government has not actually engaged in warfare against citizens of the United States on the seas, and I take the liberty, for the present at least, of postponing a discussion of our relations with the authorities at Vienna. We enter this war only where we are clearly forced into it because there are no other means of defending our rights.

It will be all the easier for us to conduct ourselves as belligerents in a high spirit of right and fairness because we act without animus, not in enmity towards a people or with the desire to bring any injury or disadvantage upon them, but only in armed opposition to an irresponsible government which has thrown aside all considerations of humanity and of right and is running amuck. We are, let me say again, the sincere friends of the German people, and shall desire nothing so much as the early reestablishment of intimate relations of mutual advantage between us—however hard it may be for them, for the time being, to believe that this is spoken from our hearts. We have borne with their present government through all these bitter months because of that friendship—exercising a patience and forbearance which would otherwise have been impossible. We shall, happily, still have an opportunity to prove that friendship in our daily attitude and actions towards the millions of men and women of German birth and native sympathy, who live amongst us and share our life, and we shall be proud to prove it towards all who are in fact loyal to their neighbours and to the Government in the hour of test. They are, most of them, as true and loyal Americans as if they had never known any other fealty or allegiance. They will be prompt to stand with us in rebuking and restraining the few who may be of a different mind and purpose. If there should be disloyalty, it will be dealt with with a firm hand of stern repression; but, if it lifts its head at all, it will lift it only here and there and without countenance except from a lawless and malignant few.

It is a distressing and oppressive duty, gentlemen of the Congress, which I have performed in thus addressing you. There are, it may be, many months of fiery trial and sacrifice ahead of us. It is a fearful thing to lead this great peaceful people into war, into the most terrible and disastrous of all wars, civilization itself seeming to be in the balance. But the right is more precious than peace, and we shall fight for the things which we have always carried nearest our hearts—for democracy, for the right of those who submit to authority to have a voice in their own governments for the rights and liberties of small nations, for a universal dominion of right by such a concert of free peoples as shall bring peace and safety to all nations and make the world itself at last free. To such a task we can dedicate our lives and our fortunes, everything that we are and everything that we have, with the pride of those who know that the day has come when America is privileged to spend her blood and her might for the principles that gave her birth and happiness and the peace which she has treasured. God helping her, she can do no other.

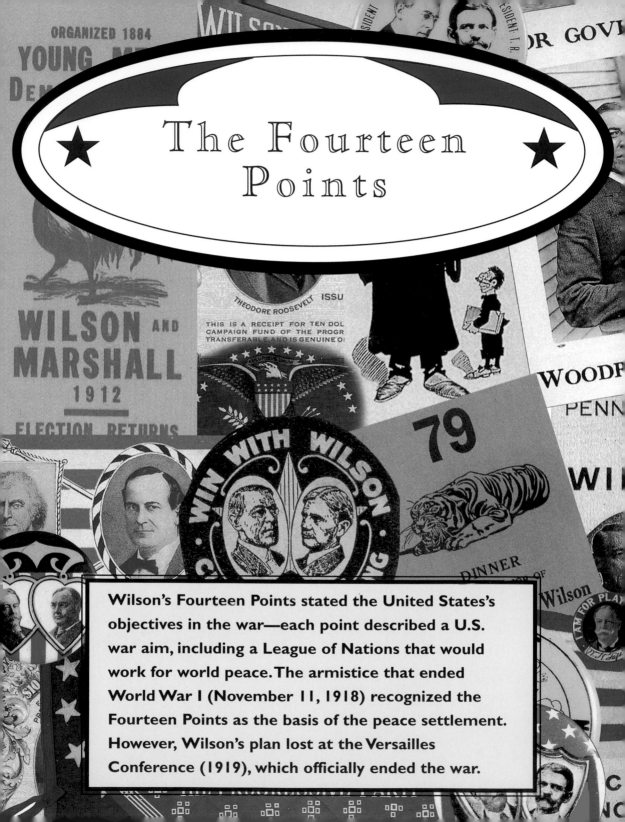

The Fourteen Points

Wilson's Fourteen Points stated the United States's objectives in the war—each point described a U.S. war aim, including a League of Nations that would work for world peace. The armistice that ended World War I (November 11, 1918) recognized the Fourteen Points as the basis of the peace settlement. However, Wilson's plan lost at the Versailles Conference (1919), which officially ended the war.

It will be our wish and purpose that the processes of peace, when they are begun, shall be absolutely open and that they shall involve and permit henceforth no secret understandings of any kind. The day of conquest and aggrandizement is gone by; so is also the day of secret covenants entered into in the interest of particular governments and likely at some unlooked-for moment to upset the peace of the world. It is this happy fact, now clear to the view of every public man whose thoughts do not still linger in an age that is dead and gone, which makes it possible for every nation whose purposes are consistent with justice and the peace of the world to avow now or at any other time the objects it has in view.

We entered this war because violations of right had occurred which touched us to the quick and made the life of our own people impossible unless they were corrected and the world secured once for all against their recurrence. What we demand in this war, therefore, is nothing peculiar to ourselves. It is that the world be made fit and safe to live in; and particularly that it be made safe for every peace-loving nation which, like our own, wishes to live its own life, determine its own institutions, be assured of justice and fair dealing by the other peoples of the world as against force and selfish aggression. All the peoples of the world are in effect partners in this interest, and for our own part we see very clearly that unless justice be done to others it will not be done to us. The program of the world's peace, therefore, is our program; and that program, the only possible program, as we see it, is this:

I. Open covenants of peace, openly arrived at, after which there shall be no private international understandings of any kind but diplomacy shall proceed always frankly and in the public view.

II. Absolute freedom of navigation upon the seas, outside territorial waters, alike in peace and in war, except as the seas may be closed in whole or in part by international action for the enforcement of international covenants.

III. The removal, so far as possible, of all economic barriers and the establishment of an equality of trade conditions among all the nations consenting to the peace and associating themselves for its maintenance.

IV. Adequate guarantees given and taken that national armaments will be reduced to the lowest point consistent with domestic safety.

V. A free, open-minded, and absolutely impartial adjustment of all colonial claims, based upon a strict observance of the principle that in determining all such questions of sovereignty the interests of the populations concerned must have equal weight with the equitable claims of the government whose title is to be determined.

VI. The evacuation of all Russian territory and such a settlement of all questions affecting Russia as will secure the best and freest cooperation of the other nations of the world in obtaining for her an unhampered and unembarrassed opportunity for the independent determination of her own political development and national policy and assure her of a sincere welcome into the society of free nations under institutions of her own choosing; and, more than a welcome, assistance also of every kind that she may need and may herself desire. The treatment accorded Russia by her sister nations in the months to come will be the acid test of their good will, of their comprehension of her needs as distinguished from their own interests, and of their intelligent and unselfish sympathy.

VII. Belgium, the whole world will agree, must be evacuated and restored, without any attempt to limit the sovereignty which she enjoys in common with all other free nations. No other single act will serve as this will serve to restore confidence among the nations in the laws which they have themselves set and determined for the government of their relations with one another. Without this healing act the whole structure and validity of international law is forever impaired.

VIII. All French territory should be freed and the invaded portions restored, and the wrong done to France by Prussia in 1871 in the matter of Alsace-Lorraine, which has unsettled the peace of the world for nearly fifty years, should be righted, in order that peace may once more be made secure in the interest of all.

IX. A readjustment of the frontiers of Italy should be effected along clearly recognizable lines of nationality.

X. The peoples of Austria-Hungary, whose place among the nations we wish to see safeguarded and assured, should be accorded the freest opportunity of autonomous development.

XI. Rumania, Serbia, and Montenegro should be evacuated; occupied territories restored; Serbia accorded free and secure access to the sea; and the relations of the several Balkan states to one another determined by friendly counsel along historically established lines of allegiance and nationality; and international guarantees of the political and economic independence and territorial integrity of the several Balkan states should be entered into.

XII. The Turkish portions of the present Ottoman Empire should be assured a secure sovereignty, but the other nationalities which are now under Turkish rule should be assured an undoubted security of life and an absolutely unmolested opportunity of an autonomous development, and the Dardanelles should be permanently opened as a free passage to the ships and commerce of all nations under international guarantees.

XIII. An independent Polish state should be erected which should include the territories inhabited by indisputably Polish populations, which should be assured a free and secure access to the sea, and whose political and economic independence and territorial integrity should be guaranteed by international covenant.

XIV. A general association of nations must be formed under specific covenants for the purpose of affording mutual guarantees of political independence and territorial integrity to great and small states alike.

In regard to these essential rectifications of wrong and assertions of right we feel ourselves to be intimate partners of all the governments and peoples associated together against the Imperialists. We cannot be separated in interest or divided in purpose. We stand together until the end.

For such arrangements and covenants we are willing to fight and to continue to fight until they are achieved; but only because we wish the right to prevail and desire a just and stable peace such as can be secured only by removing the chief provocations to war, which this program does not remove. We have no jealousy of German greatness, and there is nothing in this program that impairs it. We grudge her no achievement or distinction of learning or of pacific enterprise such as have made her record very bright and very enviable. We do not wish to injure her or to block in any way her legitimate influence or power. We do not wish to fight her either with arms or with hostile arrangements of trade if she is willing to associate herself with us and the other peace-loving nations of the world in covenants of justice and law and fair dealing. We wish her only to accept a place of equality among the peoples of the world—the new world in which we now live—instead of a place of mastery.

Neither do we presume to suggest to her any alteration or modification of her institutions. But it is necessary, we must frankly say, and necessary as a preliminary to any intelligent dealings with her on our part, that we should know whom her spokesmen speak for when they speak to us, whether for the Reichstag majority or for the military party and the men whose creed is imperial domination.

We have spoken now, surely, in terms too concrete to admit of any further doubt or question. An evident principle runs through the whole program I have outlined. It is the principle of justice to all peoples and nationalities, and their right to live on equal terms of liberty and safety with one another, whether they be strong or weak. Unless this principle be made its foundation no part of the structure of international justice can stand. The people of the United States could act upon no other principle; and to the vindication of this principle they are ready to devote their lives, their honor, and everything that they possess. The moral climax of this the culminating and final war for human liberty has come, and they are ready to put their own strength, their own highest purpose, their own integrity and devotion to the test.

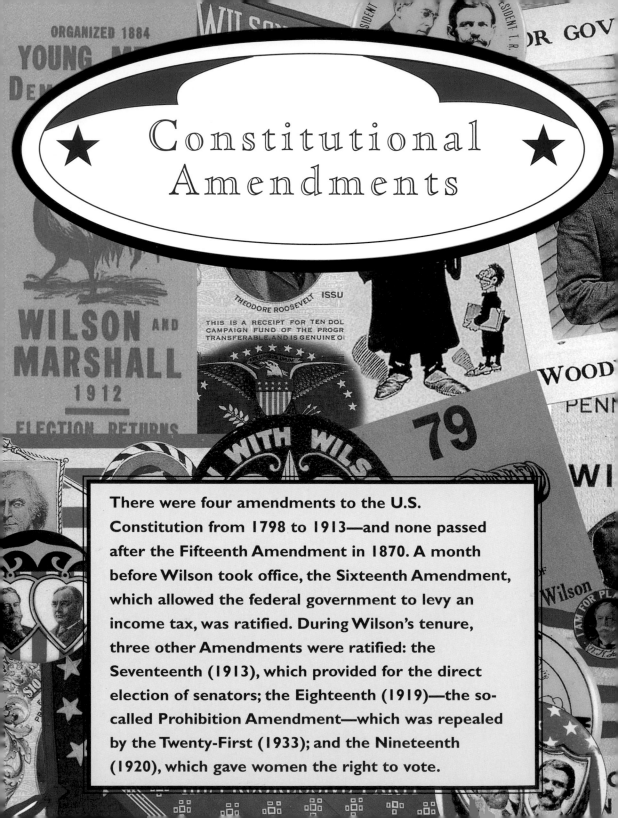

Constitutional Amendments

There were four amendments to the U.S. Constitution from 1798 to 1913—and none passed after the Fifteenth Amendment in 1870. A month before Wilson took office, the Sixteenth Amendment, which allowed the federal government to levy an income tax, was ratified. During Wilson's tenure, three other Amendments were ratified: the Seventeenth (1913), which provided for the direct election of senators; the Eighteenth (1919)—the so-called Prohibition Amendment—which was repealed by the Twenty-First (1933); and the Nineteenth (1920), which gave women the right to vote.

Seventeenth Amendment

The Senate of the United States shall be composed of two Senators from each State, elected by the people thereof, for six years; and each Senator shall have one vote. The electors in each State shall have the qualifications requisite for electors of the most numerous branch of the State legislatures.

When vacancies happen in the representation of any State in the Senate, the executive authority of such State shall issue writs of election to fill such vacancies: Provided, That the legislature of any State may empower the executive thereof to make temporary appointments until the people fill the vacancies by election as the legislature may direct.

This amendment shall not be so construed as to affect the election or term of any Senator chosen before it becomes valid as part of the Constitution.

Eighteenth Amendment

After one year from the ratification of this article the manufacture, sale, or transportation of intoxicating liquors within, the importation thereof into, or the exportation thereof from the United States and all territory subject to the jurisdiction thereof for beverage purposes is hereby prohibited.

The Congress and the several States shall have concurrent power to enforce this article by appropriate legislation. [. . .]

Nineteenth Amendment

The right of citizens of the United States to vote shall not be denied or abridged by the United States or by any State on account of sex.

Congress shall have power to enforce this article by appropriate legislation.

Further READING

GENERAL REFERENCE

Israel, Fred L. *Student's Atlas of American Presidential Elections, 1789–1996*. Washington, D.C.: Congressional Quarterly Books, 1998.

Levy, Peter B., editor. *100 Key Documents in American History*. Westport, Conn.: Praeger, 1999.

Mieczkowski, Yarek. *The Routledge Historical Atlas of Presidential Elections*. New York: Routledge, 2001.

Polsby, Nelson W., and Aaron Wildavsky. *Presidential Elections: Strategies and Structures of American Politics*. 10th edition. New York: Chatham House, 2000.

Watts, J. F., and Fred L. Israel, editors. *Presidential Documents*. New York: Routledge, 2000.

Widmer, Ted. *The New York Times Campaigns: A Century of Presidential Races*. New York: DK Publishing, 2000.

POLITICAL AMERICANA REFERENCE

Cunningham, Noble E. Jr. *Popular Images of the Presidency: From Washington to Lincoln*. Columbia: University of Missouri Press, 1991.

Melder, Keith. *Hail to the Candidate: Presidential Campaigns from Banners to Broadcasts*. Washington, D.C.: Smithsonian Institution Press, 1992.

Schlesinger, Arthur M. Jr., Fred L. Israel, and David J. Frent. *Running for President: The Candidates and their Images*. 2 vols. New York: Simon and Schuster, 1994.

Warda, Mark. *100 Years of Political Campaign Collectibles*. Clearwater, Fla.: Galt Press, 1996.

THE ELECTION OF 1912
and the Administration of Woodrow Wilson

Auchincloss, Louis. *Woodrow Wilson*. New York: Viking Press, 2000.

Brands, H. W. *T.R.: The Last Romantic*. New York: Basic Books, 1998.

Broderick, Francis L. *Progressivism at Risk: Electing a President in 1912*.
     Westport, Conn.: Greenwood Publishing Group, 1989.

Clements, Kendrick A. *Woodrow Wilson: World Statesman*. Chicago: Ivan R.
     Dee, 1999

Ginger, Ray. *The Bending Cross: A Biography of Eugene Victor Debs*.
     Kirksville, Mo.: Truman State University Press, 1992.

Keegan, John. *An Illustrated History of the First World War*. New York:
     Knopf, 2001.

Kendall, Kathleen E. *Communication in the Presidential Primaries:
     Candidates and the Media, 1912–2000*. Westport, Conn.: Praeger
     Publishing, 2000.

Morris, Edmund. *Theodore Rex*. New York: Random House, 2001.

Preston, Diana. *Lusitania: An Epic Tragedy*. New York: Walker & Co., 2002.

Pringle, Henry F. *The Life and Times of William Howard Taft*. New York:
     American Political Biography Press, 1998.

Strachan, Hew. *The First World War: To Arms*. New York: Oxford University
     Press, 2001.

White, William Allen. *Woodrow Wilson: The Man, His Times, and His Task*.
     New York: Simon Publications, 2001.

INDEX

Numbers in **bold italics** refer to captions.

The EDITORS

ARTHUR M. SCHLESINGER JR. holds the Albert Schweitzer Chair in the Humanities at the Graduate Center of the City University of New York. He is the author of more than a dozen books, including *The Age of Jackson; The Vital Center; The Age of Roosevelt* (3 vols.); *A Thousand Days: John F. Kennedy in the White House; Robert Kennedy and His Times; The Cycles of American History;* and *The Imperial Presidency.* Professor Schlesinger served as Special Assistant to President Kennedy (1961–63). His numerous awards include: the Pulitzer Prize for History; the Pulitzer Prize for Biography; two National Book Awards; The Bancroft Prize; and the American Academy of Arts and Letters Gold Medal for History.

FRED L. ISRAEL is professor emeritus of American history, City College of New York. He is the author of *Nevada's Key Pittman* and has edited *The War Diary of Breckinridge Long* and *Major Peace Treaties of Modern History, 1648–1975* (5 vols.) He holds the Scribe's Award from the American Bar Association for his joint editorship of the *Justices of the United States Supreme Court* (4 vols.). For more than 25 years Professor Israel has compiled and edited the Gallup Poll into annual reference volumes.

DAVID J. FRENT is the president of Political Americana Auctions, Oakhurst, NJ. With his wife, Janice, he has assembled the nation's foremost private collection of political campaign memorabilia. Mr. Frent has designed exhibits for corporations, the Smithsonian Institution, and the United States Information Agency. A member of the board of directors of the American Political Items Collectors since 1972, he was elected to its Hall of Fame for his "outstanding contribution to preserving and studying our political heritage."